A VOICE ACTOR'S GUIDE TO AUDIO DESCRIPTION PERFORMANCE:

Crafting Immersive Entertainment Experiences for Blind Audiences

by

Roy Samuelson

NIBI PRESS

Published by
Nibi Press, LLC | Los Angeles, CA
NibiPress.com

Library of Congress Control Number:
Paperback ISBN: 979-8-9853342-2-7
Ebook ISBN: 979-8-9853342-3-4
Audiobook ISBN: 979-8-9853342-4-1
Printed in the USA
First Edition 2024
Edited by Vivian Syroyezhkin
Edited by Brett Paesel
Copy Edited by Lisa Burrell
Sensitivity Read by Rebecca Odum
Cover Art and Layout by Christin Lee

To you.

For your kindness,
vulnerability,
and understanding.

)))

TABLE OF CONTENTS

)))

FORWARD
Stating the Obvious

Equity, parity, equality, and inclusion are often tossed around like interchangeable terms but, while they're all noble pursuits, they're as different as apples and zebras.

Let's start with **equality**. Imagine a concert where everyone's seat is at the same height. Seems fair, right? Well, not quite. That's the problem with equality: it assumes everyone starts from the same place. But we all know that's not true. Some folks are born taller/stronger/wealthier/smarter, while others are struggling to make ends meet.

That's where **equity** comes in. Equity is about recognizing that we all have diverse needs and providing the support necessary to ensure everyone has a fair shot at success. It's like giving everyone the tools they need to build their own house, rather than just giving everyone the same house.

Parity, on the other hand, is about achieving equal outcomes. It's not just about ensuring everyone has the same opportunities, but also ensuring that everyone ends up in the same place. It's like making sure everyone finishes the race at the same time, regardless of their starting point. This may not be useful in a competitive experience, but then enjoying conventional lean-back filmed or TV entertainment is not supposed to be a competitive experience, is it?

I am not suggesting that those with advantages should lose their gifts. Instead, we need to recognize and address that these advantages have historically prevented others from fully realizing their potential. A small shift in our perspective can significantly broaden our understanding. We all have biases, whether conscious or unconscious, and these biases are not limited to the privileged or racist among us. Unconscious biases, in particular, can profoundly impact our interactions and prevent entire sectors of society from experiencing life equitably. So, what can we do about this?

This foreword isn't the place for such a complex discussion. Instead, I encourage you to explore that important topic separately. For now, I'll focus on briefly highlighting Roy Samuelson's work and how this publication serves as an example of his admirable contributions.

Roy, like all good actors, is an artist. He channels his emotions and voice to create and share experiences. My professional association with him these past several years has proven his commitment to an ideal wherein shared experiences ought to be moments absorbed by all participants, in parity. These experiences should be within the reach of all, irrespective of our functional differences. Roy believes that great entertainment meets us not where we function, but where we feel. Roy approaches his craft, his industry, and the challenges we still face with a generosity of spirit rare in today's competitive landscape. His example gives us permission to reframe our perspective on and thereby our activities within this industry, and perhaps grow into a new era of productive collaboration, inclusive creativity, and shared prosperity.

While this book was conceived as a primer for AD professionals, it is something more than the sum of its chapters. The insights that Roy shares provide sighted audiences with a rare education in what life can be like when one faces hurdles to accessibility and equity.

Every AD performer who reads this book will have several "I feel seen, at last!" moments. Perhaps more valuable is the fact that you will have as many "aha!" moments, when you finally understand something that has nagged you for months, or even years, but only now is being codified in language that allows you to identify and advocate for yourself and your professional peers.

This book provides not only time-proven techniques for better performance, but priceless tips and resources for Voice-Over and AD performers of all stripes.

I have spent nearly my entire life in the entertainment industry, starting in theatre and moving on to film and TV, with a significant stint in the dynamic world of video games and interactive digital entertainment. Throughout my journey, I've built technologies, companies, industry alliances, and more. I've faced numerous challenges and obstacles, often unaware of how my privilege or the favorable biases of others contributed to my successes. Recently, disability and other experiences have led me into unexpected chapters of my life. Despite the difficult aspects of these experiences, they have also brought me invaluable insights, relationships, lessons, and opportunities that emerged through these struggles.

My father was recently diagnosed with irreversible vision loss. He shared with me his journey through anger, resistance, acceptance, and even depression. Now, he is beginning to find new options, thanks to the support of an extraordinary and diverse community, of which he is a new member. Emotions can be contradictory yet coexistent, much like life itself. When we encounter people who strive to make this dichotomy more livable, accessible, and equitable, we should listen to them and amplify their voices. They work on behalf of others, which is the noblest endeavor. Making room for others does not diminish our own space; instead, it enriches the environment in which we all grow and flourish.

I am eager to learn how this book helps you to flourish and realize your fullest potential, be it as an artist, a technician, an executive, or an audience member. **We are each a part of the narrative.**

Nicholas de Wolff
https://about.me/dewolff/

)))

Defining AD?

To liven up your commute, you've downloaded the audio version of a great book. You settle in and hit play.

But in the first sentence—ugh—you hear THAT VOICE. It's grating on your nerves. The over-enunciated words. The high-handed tone. But you try really, *really* hard to give it a listen, thinking, "I'll get over it. It's one of my favorite books."

You just can't, though. After barely making it through the first few sentences, you know that even thirty more seconds would be torture. You switch over to radio, resigned to another same-old commute—annoyed that you've wasted an Audible credit.

When you get to work, you delete the file, wishing you lived in an alternate universe where you could hear this book the way you've heard many great audiobooks before. Why does this one have to be so...*unlistenable?*

If you're a voice performer yourself, you actually know what's missing: subtlety. Performing an audiobook isn't just about reading the written word aloud so it can be captured on a sound file. It's a craft. It requires nuance.

The same is true of performing audio description (AD)—that is, translating entertainment media into something that everyone, not just sighted, can fully enjoy. In this book, we'll talk about the inherent challenges and what it takes to deliver the immersive experience that the story and the audience both deserve.

While primarily for AD performers in film and TV, this book also covers other aspects of AD that affect performance—the writing, the sound engineering, and more. We don't work in a vacuum.

My hopes for you, wherever you are in your life and career:

- If you're new to AD and interested in doing the work, or even just curious about how it comes together, please bring your assumptions. I hope that they will be watermelons to this AD Gallagher.[1]

- If you work in the broader field of accessibility or want to do so, I hope you'll find insights within this AD microcosm that you can apply to the situations and challenges in your sector.

- I also hope to show anyone who might see AD work as "checking a box" (doing the bare minimum requirements) the benefits of going far beyond bare-minimum requirements to create more immersive experiences for our audiences.

- Finally, if you *already* work in AD or use it regularly: I'm on your side. I understand there are many perspectives on AD, and mine may not

---

1 Google "Gallagher watermelons," and you're welcome.

fully align with yours (we're human beings! with different experiences and ideas!). I hope this guide will still enhance what you intuitively know and maybe plant some new seeds for professional growth. As an AD performer myself, I sympathize with your predicaments and appreciate your quiet accomplishments. I celebrate your public successes, too! Even if we don't talk or haven't talked for a long time, or ever, I hope you see this book as a letter of loyalty to you. I want you to feel seen *and* heard.

The AD industry in film and TV is changing in varying ways and at various speeds. Within a matter of months, some things, such as the technology we use and the particular audiences we're able to reach, will have already changed. Other factors, like the human needs we want to meet and the access we try to provide, will remain very much the same. My goal here is to share what I've learned so far during a decade of doing AD work so that together—whether you're an AD performer,[2] AD writer, AD producer, entertainment executive, audience member, or someone who is simply AD curious at this point—*we can set and meet the highest expectations for quality.*

Before we get started, though, I should address any confusion there might be on a critical point:

What is audio description, anyway? I mean, I sort of—briefly—defined the concept above. But did that give you a concrete sense of what's involved?

No? I'm not surprised.

The FCC defines audio description as: "The insertion of au-

---

2 Why not "narrator"? Or "voicer"? "Voice actor" or "voice talent"? Because none of these labels fully captures the work involved. After dozens of conversations and devil's-advocate games of logic with colleagues and friends in the industry, I've decided that the term "AD performer" sums it up.

dio-narrated descriptions of a television program's key visual elements into natural pauses in the program's dialogue."[3]

For our purposes, here's a more user-focused way of looking at it: *AD in entertainment is a way for people on the blindness spectrum to enjoy all visuals in an immersive experience—in parity with sighted audiences.*

That seems clearer, but it's still pretty general, isn't it? *How* can AD create an immersive experience for the audience? In what ways does it fall short? And how can we make it better? These are the sorts of questions I grapple with as the host of *The ADNA Presents* podcast, in interviews with people from all walks of AD life.[4] Throughout this book I draw on many such conversations, for example the one I had with Hannah Waymouth, a blind social media influencer who both relies on and enjoys AD. Here's her take on what AD means and does, particularly for audiences who are new to it:

> At first, it was kind of jarring. But once you got used to it, it was amazing. It took a couple of episodes and then I was like, I get the gist of this. It was the most amazing thing ever.
>
> ...when I've turned it on with anyone sighted around me, they have a hard time with it because, yeah, it is redundant; you're seeing everything that's happening [and hearing it, too]. But, I got more and more used to it. The less and less I could see, even when I still had vision, the more I allowed my eyes to relax and not sit there and try to focus on everything.

---

3 I get grumpy when AD is inexplicably pluralized as "audio descriptions," which somehow sounds as though it's a grocery store product.

4 https://theadna.org/the-adna-presents/

It then just, it just seemed to flow.[5]

That initially jarring experience Waymouth describes is fairly common, because there's often a chaotic feel to AD for film and TV. But in my experience and research, I've seen a pattern in the chaos: Much of it stems from having so many different (unsystematic) approaches out there to every aspect of AD. So, when I'm asked, "What is audio description?" I like to respond with a diatribe along these lines, written like a poem.

What is Audio Description for Film and TV?[6]

Oh, in the world of audio description

(also called video description, or descriptive video, or descriptive narration),

a describer [7]

(who might be the writer? or performer? or maybe it's both the writer and performer? or maybe it's the company? but not the production company or the distributor, but a special other

---

5 Audio quotes throughout are lightly edited for clarity. You can listen to this interview here: https://www.roysamuelson.com/interviews/hannah-waymouth/

6 I wrote this bit for a keynote speech at the American Council of the Blind's 2020 conference. You can hear the whole thing on the "Roy Samuelson" episode of The ADNA Presents podcast: https://www.roysamuelson.com/interviews/roy-samuelson/ and another live performance of the 3 minutes at https://www.roysamuelson.com/comic-con-panel-2024/

7 Like "voice talent" and other terms I tend to avoid when describing the people who do AD, "describer" waters things down, in my view. It also implies that AD work is a technical one-person gig rather than a rich collaboration.

company?)

captures visual elements of a film or TV show on a split track. Or mix track.

If the film or show even has it.

Which depends on:
the distribution channel
(like streaming, theatrical, broadcast, physical like Blu-ray or DVD, or downloadable to iTunes, or Google Play, or YouTube)

which can offer varying levels of access to the audio description,

whether
on an app
or on a TV
or on a cable box
or on a browser with a special plug-in,
or on YouTube.

Maybe it's a separate YouTube video with audio description!

But!

Maybe the audio description's separately downloadable and it syncs up,

and then you listen to:
a performer,
or a synth voice that sounds like "a conversational robot,"
or maybe it's a performer that sounds like a synth voice.

But you don't know if the audio description is there until you

hear it,
which could be a few minutes into the show,
so you wait and wait and hope
and then...

You don't hear it.

So you have to decide to stop and complain
or just put up with it.

But if you do decide to complain,
who do you complain to?

Is it the local broadcast affiliate,

or the movie theater manager, dealing with Karen's complaint
about her unpopped popcorn kernel,

or do you contact one of the 47-plus streaming services,

by email?
message?
...Fax? Or Facebook?
Tweet?
Phone?

But to FIND that phone, you have to hunt down a number;

And once you find that number,
you go through a press-one, press-three, sorry-your-call-
cannot-be-completed-as-dialed?

Or try a different number, and—is that the main line?

Ugh, another press-4, press-0, holding…

Oh good—you can talk to a real person! And it goes something like this:

"Uhhm, yes, my speakers are working."

"No, audio description isn't closed captioning."

"Sure, I'll hold."

Or—is it better to go through an accessibility web link? Buried so deep it feels like they don't want to talk to you.

And even when the audio description is there, and it's bad— what does that even mean?

Is the writing indicating things the visuals don't have?

Does the AD performer of a scary, suspenseful movie talk to you like you are a baby toddler?

Does a kids' show have an uninterested adult performing AD, who sounds as tasteless as cereal too long in the milk?

Or: Is it just that aforementioned synth voice my friend Melody calls "a puppet."

Or: Even creepy, like a horror monster, made to describe the lighthearted comedy romance film to you!

And who chose that voice, and why?

Does that voice get in the way of your experience?

And do you have to keep fiddling with the volume —

up
and down
and down
and down
and up,

to try to hear it, depending on what's going on in the background?

Or maybe the production audio

                           ducks down, out of the way —

so you can hear the performer, but the other audio disappears, and it's jarring and it takes you out of the story?

And does this work

that is created for blind people,

actually

include

blind
people

in

the

process?

....mmmmm Maybe?

———

So much for a clear definition of audio description.

I really wish I could provide one. But since the industry itself is still feeling its way toward what AD should be, it's highly inconsistent from project to project—and from audience experience to audience experience. Given all the variables, there are *so many things* that can go awry at each step of the AD-creation process.

We'll talk about some of those things.[8]

---

8 OOOOoooo I'm getting excited to share this book with you! And one more thing — English teachers beware! I use commas, parentheses, and dashes to indicate pauses, and slow you down. I use this convention in my AD scripts, and you might find it an unusual reading experience. Here we go!

A VOICE ACTOR'S GUIDE TO AUDIO DESCRIPTION PERFORMANCE:

Crafting Immersive Entertainment Experiences for Blind Audiences

———————

))

INTRODUCTION
Pivoting from How Cheap to How Great

Why would you read a book about accessibility in entertainment media that was written by a sighted voiceover (VO) actor? Because I've learned a lot through my work experience, and I'm deeply committed to making it better. In addition to the thousands of audio description projects I've performed, I've collaborated closely with AD pros and entertainment executives both to improve AD quality and to secure opportunities for blind performers.

Since 1992, I've been paid to speak words into a microphone. Starting with a voiceover role as a gangster in a Disney theme park attraction,[1] I then moved on to doing VO for Super Bowl commercials and video game characters, making swallowing noises for celebrities, and then, in 2014, performing audio description – an area on which I have focused most of

---

1 Search YouTube for "great movie ride gangster disney studios." In my role, I enjoyed hijacking a vehicle and getting blown up every 7 minutes.

my professional attention ever since.

Though I didn't realize it at the time, I began "training" for that AD work in 2006, when I shifted to VO freelancing and a friend—a talented on-camera actor—invited me to a writers' group meeting. I was confused. Why would a voice actor do a writers' group?

My friend explained that this particular group of a few dozen writers for film and TV invited actors like me to come in and read scripts every week. Four of the writers would each bring in 25 pages of their work. After listening to the actors read, all the writers would give feedback on the writing.

I loved the idea and started going weekly. As an actor, I wanted to bring my best work, and so I put a lot of energy into my performance. But I also quickly realized that this wasn't about me. Our job was to focus on the story being told and not on getting in the way of that story.

With that shared goal, the many actors who attended these meetings brought the scenes and characters to life. In the process, we learned a great deal—both about writing and about our craft as performers.

We didn't just read the lines of dialogue; we also read the stage directions laying out the action sequences and everything else that would appear on screen. I saw so much value in hearing the script. It allowed the writers to fully immerse themselves in what was happening simply by listening.

After 10 years of meeting nearly every week, I was reading words without preparation: I picked up on cold-reading technique. And somewhere along the way, one of my actor friends from that group introduced me to audio description work. When I asked what that was like, she shared the skills required, many of which I had already developed in the writers' group—cold reading, jumping in between lines of dialogue, and maintaining a nuanced, story-supporting focus.

An AD performer was born.

Soon after, I went to an AD audition and saw the behind-the-scenes magic: an AD script with all its information, along with the other audio and visuals of a TV series. I jumped in and out between the characters speaking (like a veteran "dialogue dodger").

After the audition, I couldn't get any sleep that night. Of course I was excited about booking the job. But I was also excited about being introduced to a genre of voiceover performance that had so many satisfying elements—so many ways of supporting the story.

I was all in.

Connecting with Audiences Who Often Feel Isolated

"Audio description enthusiast" Renee VanAusdall, has this to say on The ADNA Presents podcast about her experience with AD:

> As someone who is blind, audio description lets me into the experience of watching a movie. I feel less isolated, which I think is probably a very common feeling for people who are limited in what they can see. So, for me, it feels like it's that connection to the thing I'm enjoying.[2]

That experience of connection she describes—much too rare for blind film and TV audiences—has always been the driving force behind my desire to make AD the best it can be. It's been a journey, collaborating with like-minded artists to create the strongest AD work we can and modeling what that might look like for others in the entertainment industry.

---

2 https://www.roysamuelson.com/interviews/renee-vanausdall/

En route, I've spent much of my time training, doing practice workouts for my voice, being coached, and auditioning and booking jobs through my voiceover agents. I approach all that work, both the preparing and the performing, with a strong bias toward bringing *intention* to the story.

As a voiceover actor, in AD and otherwise, *I ride that emotional wave* with the audience. To immerse them in the story, I immerse myself, taking the words I say off the page and infusing them with meaning from the heart and the gut.

That process of bringing intention to a script is what separates performances that connect us as human beings from those that...don't. Gloss over that process, or neglect it altogether, and you risk delivering the equivalent of an elementary school book report: a dull, even painful experience that's informative on some level, maybe, but far from engaging. The intention you bring to your VO work matters.

By also providing access to the *visual* intent, AD performers connect and communicate with the audience on yet another level. Their skills go way beyond clearly enunciating words and "sounding conversational."

AD has traditionally been seen as "captioning for blind people." While accessibility is an essential part of any story for audiences with disabilities, audio description is *not merely a transcription of visual content into audio form*. Rather, it's *an adaptation of a script*—and thus a creation in its own right, with its own casting, recording, editing, mixing, directing, engineering, producing, performing, and quality control, to name a few departments.[3] In short, AD is an *entirely new production, realized in the audio realm*.

Is it always (or ever) a perfect production? No.

---

3 I've stopped using the word "roles" to label the different parts of the AD process. That got confusing in a film and TV context. And anyway, "departments" better reflects the reality that sometimes multiple people contribute within each area of expertise.

Sometimes We Miss the Mark

Sadly, some AD performers sound as though they're only reading a script—not saying the words as if they were their own, not supporting the story with their voices, not infusing it with nuance or emotion. For them, it's book report time.

Others are incredibly conversational but never vary their tone. Imagine a warm, friendly voice saying, "In the pits of hell, the woman slays the dragon," in the same tone you would reasonably expect from someone wishing you a very nice day. How distracting!

Still others are just plain over the top: shouting one minute, nearly crying the next, sounding like someone's drunk uncle watching a football game.

How can we make AD better all around? How can we help more audiences get the immersive experience sighted people simply take for granted?

We can start by treating audio description as a way *into* the story. Again, Renee VanAusdall:

> So, it's not new that we get somebody from outside the story telling us things about the story— that's not new to have a narrator, right? We have movies like *The Muppet Christmas Carol*, where the narrator is the favorite part of the movie. We get instances where a narrator, like in *The Wonder Years*, tells us about the emotion of what is being experienced on the screen. Or *Young Sheldon* is another example where you have this voiceover, this narrator who is bringing you through the story. I think good audio description feels like that in-story narrator, giving you sort of these clues about all the other things that you're experiencing, the dialogue, the diegetic sound,

all of those other parts of it. You are getting more information from this person who is part of the story too. *If it's done well.*

When I embarked on a career in AD, I was looking for a way to *perform as an integrated narrator*. I wanted to tap the emotion of a scene without distracting audiences from the events I was describing. Striking that balance was important. An inappropriately performed AD script actually changes the content for the worse.

A focus on accessibility shouldn't lead to subpar performances, and yet, I began to notice, it often did. Why was the industry sacrificing the emotional experience of the audience? Why did all the exciting opportunities to provide great AD, thanks to a tsunami of new entertainment content, so quickly become exercises in box-checking?

AD in film and TV was starting to feel like a race to the bottom.[4]

Turning that race around would take more than just awareness, I realized. Once producers and directors turned their attention to AD, most tried to get it done with the least amount of cost and fuss. As a result, they missed opportunities to add creative value to their productions. Or, to put it another way:

Cheapening this work devalued the story.

Making matters worse, talented AD performers left the business because it wasn't sustainable for them to continue and support themselves or their families. With more amateurs entering the field, loud and brash voices (and, on the opposite end, flat word-readers) became commonplace.

Even with good intentions of "helping blind people," the industry cut corners, which established a lower tier of acceptability.

---

4 I'm not pointing fingers or trying to shame anyone here. It was — and remains — a gnarly problem to solve.

At the end of the day, the audience experience for blind people is so much less than what sighted people are getting. AD audiences were put in the position of saying, "Well, at least we have AD" — as if that was enough.

Delivering AD that doesn't match the quality of the original content amounts to discrimination. Most people think discrimination is a clear-cut lack of accessibility. For example: There either is or isn't a ramp for a wheelchair. There either is or isn't closed captioning. There either is or isn't AD.

That's not how discrimination works.

Renee VanAusdall likens it to slapping a wheelchair ramp onto a building with no regard for the architecture, when "everybody else gets this grand buildup with the staircase." She adds: "Sometimes we have to go around the back because that's where the accessible entrance is, and I know that we miss out on some things that way."

A poorly designed or poorly built accommodation may well be an effort to give blind and sighted audiences the same quality of experience. But if it's not working that way, it's still discriminatory.

The thing is, AD *can* bring audiences along for an immersive ride. Why doesn't it do that more often?

The FCC mandates that theatrical releases and certain cable stations provide AD. (Note that streaming services are, at the time of this writing, exempt from this requirement, although some have preemptively opted into AD.) But when the goal is to check the box, anything beyond the box becomes unnecessary. Yes, we offer "accessibility." But we don't give people *equitable* access to high-quality experiences. That's a creative failure as well as a commercial failure.

As movie reviewer John Stark pointed out:

> ...we deserve to not only watch any title we want, like sighted people can, but it is a reasonable ask

for that audio description to be worthy of being on the work of art to which it is attached.[5]

The entertainment industry has a compelling "why" for creating high-quality AD. *But the "how" is missing (and so are practical incentives for making the "how" happen).*

For starters, we need more consistency—but not enforced dictums: a balanced approach, one that allows for subjectivity, creativity, and flexibility.

Let's Bust Some Silos

As of this writing, audio description in film and TV remains wildly inconsistent from project to project: One series might not have AD at all. Another might invite the AD writer to the shooting set. Sometimes, TV and film producers set expectations for AD facilities. Other times, distributors outsource AD to companies that might subcontract to other companies, that might—in turn—hire freelancers who have no experience in audio, let alone accessibility.

The logistics are all over the place. And that's not even beginning to address the wide range of creative approaches to AD, pay rates, timing turnarounds, and so on.

What do we call these wide-ranging inconsistencies? For over a decade, I've used the "Wild West" analogy. But maybe a more apt comparison is the Tower of Babel.

In the AD world, we sometimes speak different languages—or use the same language to mean different things. With the rapid rate of creation in entertainment media, those layers of meaning don't have much time to sync up, which can lead to misunderstandings.

---

5 https://macthemovieguy.com/2024/01/06/foe-the-review-to-end-all-reviews/

Within that chaos, we have many silos: different AD facilities, departments, and contributors don't interact much, so they don't often ask one another questions or share knowledge about their respective jobs. There's also a disconnect between the actual original production team and the AD facilities and their teams. The people in these various silos may miss the big picture or cling to assumptions that might not work in other AD areas.

That's not to say we should all approach AD work in exactly the same way. If we did, we'd sacrifice creativity.

Yet, ensuring quality does require a certain level of agreement about what works best. And it involves interacting with and learning from others in the business who inspire you to do better work.

Better AD Sparks Human Connection

A dear friend of mine and I watched the first season of a comedy series together. We laughed, judged, relived the one-liners, and talked about our favorite characters and what they did. He was a screenwriter, so he particularly loved the storytelling, and I loved hearing his perspective on things that I had missed.

When the second season of the show came out, he was in chemo. One procedure caused permanent and total blindness.

But when I visited him in the hospital, we didn't talk much about the cancer or the care he was receiving. Instead, we talked about that funny thing that character did in the new season of our favorite show. We discussed the story's plot twists and how great the action sequence was.

AD for that show meant that my friend and I could maintain that same connection with each other we'd had before his chemo. It meant we could share observations without navigating the conversational speed bumps of "wait, what happened?" He and I had both caught the latest episode. We played a few clips with audio description together. There were touching moments where we cried together. And we laughed together.

At its best, AD—just like entertainment itself—connects us.

Here's how I put it a few years ago in the Twenty Thousand Hertz "A Thousand Words" podcast:

> I think about every time that there is an experience that I've had with a movie that moved me emotionally. The first thing I wanted to do was call one of my dear friends and share: "This is such a great experience." Or if I saw it with someone, it's that experience that is a connection. Our blind and low-vision audiences deserve that experience too.[6]

When that connection feels effortless, it is because skilled professionals have come together to put in hours of their best work in a way that not only didn't add speed bumps but made the landscaped highway a joy for all to experience.

Professionalism is Key

If the sky's the limit in other aspects of entertainment, why not take that approach with audio description? Making AD better requires an intense focus on how great, not how cheap, AD can be.

Thankfully, not everyone views it as a set of costs to cut. When investments in quality are made, the final result is that

---

6 https://www.20k.org/episodes/athousandwords

the audio description is turned on, and it seamlessly blends into the show, so that audiences aren't distracted or "taken out" of the story by lackluster AD performances, writing, or placement.

In other words, an immersive product is a professional product.

Professionalism is more than competence. For voice actors and others involved in crafting AD, it involves developing and honing specialized skills through ongoing study, coaching, and practice. It is the diligent pursuit of excellence.

It involves collaboration, too. Specifically in AD for film and TV, the efforts of multiple departments are brought to bear on the challenge of achieving parity with what sighted audiences experience. Beyond leveraging one another's skills and talents, people who do this work must build and maintain respectful relationships with one another to set and meet high standards.

Most of all, professionalism in AD is about ensuring quality, which can get lost in a mad dash for quantity. That means keeping people immersed in the story. It means releasing the AD version at the same time as the version for sighted audiences. It means ensuring that the AD track travels everywhere with the film or series, from cinema to streaming and onward.

Over the past few years, I've interviewed nearly 300 AD professionals on The ADNA Presents podcast.[7] By speaking with people across various AD departments, I've tried not only to introduce listeners to the many types of contributors in the AD world but also to highlight the merits of their different perspectives and approaches. Guests talk about their skills as well, which they've developed through years of training and work experience.

Interviews with AD pros are a rich source of ideas for better

---

7 http://theadna.org/the-adna-presents

serving AD audiences. You'll see quite a few of those ideas in this book. But before we can implement any of them on a large scale, we need to realize one key systemic change—namely, more professionalism in the AD industry as a whole.

The good news is that individuals both within and outside the industry are effecting positive change by modeling professionalism and by trying new approaches here and there. A very smart colleague of mine calls this strategy "incrementalism." We can take such steps publicly or behind the scenes. Not everyone will like every new idea. Sensibilities vary. But if we share the overall goal of bringing our AD audiences what they deserve, we can—in our many different ways, departments, venues, and projects—make progress toward that goal.

And there's so much progress to make. Even when we're preaching to the choir, we've got assumptions and biases to overcome—our own included. I'm fascinated by accessibility, and yet I've found my own limiting beliefs challenged in conversations with AD pros. As a sighted person, I'm so very grateful to amplify the voices (on mic and otherwise!) of those who have approached this work with the kind of professional alignment and consistency we need throughout the industry.

Settle for Nothing Short of Parity

Blind audiences know what they deserve when it comes to AD and how it affects their immersion. The professionals who create and produce shows and films know what story they want to tell and how they want their audiences to experience it. Those sets of goals should feed each other—and they do when AD is done right.

By making deliberate creative choices (around timing, intention, and so on), we can help blind and sighted audiences alike feel the story's full emotional impact and, therefore, experience the story in much the same way. As AD performers, we have many resources at our disposal to make those things happen—our many talented collaborators in other departments, for instance, and our investments in developing our own craft. We can't do it alone, though. We need support from above.

As computer scientist John Gruber put it in "The Auteur Theory of Design" (2009): "The quality of any creative endeavor tends to approach the level of taste of whoever is in charge."

Let's get philosophical here (Roy dusts off the soapbox and stomps both feet on top):

When directors and producers recognize the creative, economic, and other benefits of AD, they become more likely to explore new ways of making their films and shows accessible to all audiences. That's partly because understanding what AD does builds greater awareness of disability writ large; it expands their understanding of what access means. Once their assumptions about access are updated, they get curious and look for innovative ways of reaching and moving all kinds of audiences. They find new touchpoints and new tools. In the same way a curb cutout was built for wheelchair users but also accommodates people who push strollers and those who have a tough time stepping up, AD can enrich the experience of various sighted audiences as well as blind ones.

By thinking about accessibility more expansively, entertainment executives can also have a positive impact on their own crew of professionals. They can all make the work more accessible.

This is a different approach than charity or "giving back." Those things matter, of course, but in the entertainment industry (and elsewhere), they don't fix inequity.

Enhancing the film or TV experience for everyone while attending to the needs of blind audiences is a form of inclusion and parity. When all the elements and departments are working together—the writing, the performance, the sound engineering, the quality control—and when all cylinders are firing, the AD works with the rest of the film or TV show to support the story. That's when the immersive experience comes alive. That's when we can hope to achieve parity.

In this book, we'll look at some exciting contributions that can be made within—and in collaboration with—those departments. We'll draw on my experiences where I've worked with numerous AD facilities (companies hired to provide AD for movies and TV series), along with hundreds of interviews with AD professionals and audience members, to understand how these varying perspectives and sets of responsibilities inform the AD performers' work.

While this book is written principally for AD performers, both those in the industry already and those wanting to join it, we'll also look at the effects of decisions made in other areas. The context surrounding our work matters—not just the performing but also the writing, the engineering, the quality control, and industry influences. Understanding the challenges in that larger AD world, and collaborating across areas of expertise to address them, is what it takes to create a truly immersive audience experience.

We'll also discuss how each department contributes to low-quality AD. Often without realizing it, we're all guilty of creating *inaccessibilities*: roadblocks and speed bumps that prevent immersion by jolting audiences out of the story.

So, in response to the classic voiceover question, "Who are you talking to?", we'll begin by getting to know our AD audiences better. Then we can talk about your craft as an AD performer and how the choices made in other departments can affect your work. Even if you have no interest in developing those specialized skills, keeping these departments' goals and needs in mind will inevitably improve your performance. In each chapter, we'll pivot from the challenges faced to the professionalism needed to overcome them.[8]

We'll wrap up by discussing the impact you can have in bringing our AD audiences what they deserve.

Let's get started.

---

8 If you are an AD performer, you likely are a dialogue dodger, which means you're adept at jumping around audio obstacles. We also have a lot of other obstacles and challenges to navigate.

)))

CHAPTER 1
Knowing Your AD Audience

We've got two realities for AD audiences—the way things typically go, and a much better way.

First, let's talk about business as usual.

It's the Sighted Leading the Sighted

Imagine going to a movie theater with some friends. You order your popcorn and drink and settle into some seats. Then the movie starts!

But something's missing. Your friends are all laughing, crying, and gasping at the same moments, while you're left feeling…not much of anything except isolation from the action on screen and from the people around you. What are they getting that you aren't?

You go to the manager and describe your situation. You can tell what this experience should be like, based on others' reactions, but it's not happening for you. The manager gives you a shoulder shrug of an "I dunno," and a free movie pass. You go back to your seat and sit next to your friends, who are still clearly engaged in a way that eludes you. You crinkle the free pass—one more to add to the stack you've collected at home.

Our AD audiences, most of whom are on the blindness spectrum, feel this frustration more often than not. Even when AD exists, it tends to assume total blindness from birth. Individual audience members can't adjust the description "up" or "down" to meet their needs. As Hannah Waymouth (the avid AD user you met in the introduction) explains,

> People have varying degrees of blindness.
>
> And...just because you're blind doesn't mean that you were born blind. A lot of people have gone blind later in life. They've come from a sighted world to a blind world. That's a whole other thing.
>
> I used to see, and now I can't. I want to know everything [that's happening visually] because I remember what things look like. I think a lot of people have a lot of misconceptions about that.

When AD disappoints, it's often, I think, a consequence of believing we know our audiences better than we do. As a result, many of the people we are trying to reach can end up falling through the cracks.

Sometimes, our attempts to provide accessibility *create* access problems. Here are a few of the challenges that crop up.

———

Challenge 1: "How do you turn this thing on?"

Oh, technology. All those apps, websites, subfolders, aimless searches, buried settings... User experience can be rough for everyone. But it's often especially excruciating for blind people.

AD still isn't available for many titles, particularly films and series that have been around a long time. And when it does exist, simply accessing it can be a major headache. Since audio description doesn't currently travel with the rest of the production from "cinema to streaming," audiences who need it don't reliably get it. (A common complaint: "But I saw this movie with AD in a theater. Why doesn't the version I bought have AD on my TV?") Just because a movie or show has AD on one platform doesn't mean it will have the same (or any) AD elsewhere.

In the words of Juan Alcazar, a blind filmmaker and AD quality control specialist:

> [A film or show] might not even have an audio description track. Or even worse, it might actu-ally disappear... I ended up renting [a show] on iTunes since I have an Apple TV, but only after I rented it did I realize that the Peacock version had AD, not the iTunes version. That's just one of the things that is extremely irritating: a lot of times, tracks don't migrate to other streaming services.[1]

Such inconsistencies in AD access make audiences feel as though they aren't in good hands. They never know for sure if they're going to get a version of a show or movie that they can fully enjoy.

---

1 https://www.roysamuelson.com/interviews/juan-alcazar/

And once the AD is turned on, it might not stay on. That means people will have to manually turn it on again and again, sometimes for every single episode of the same show they want to binge-watch.

To make things more frustrating, episodes may be released without audio description in a series that had it in previous seasons. This isn't a big problem when episodes can stand alone. But when a story is told over multiple seasons and episodes, not having AD for some episodes, but not others, creates sizable gaps in the plot.

In movie theaters, AD audiences face other access hurdles. They might have to wait until the release date to find out if a film even has audio description. Theaters often provide cordless headsets, but employees sometimes don't understand what those AD headsets do, mistaking them for audio enhancement and handing people devices that just make everything louder.

These obstacles to access are relatively straightforward, even simple, but they're widespread—and they're not the only challenge for audiences.

Challenge 2: *So much* AD is just "meh"

Even when people can access the AD relatively easily, it won't necessarily provide an immersive, emotional experience. In fact, it usually doesn't, because of the way industry incentives are aligned.

Let's say I run an AD facility that offers a full range of services. I might charge a certain amount in the absence of competition from other facilities. But in the real world, *with* competition, I'll look for ways to provide those services more cheaply so my company can stay afloat.

There is intense pressure for AD facilities to cut costs (and corners), because AD is one of the first costs their main clients, the streaming services, will cut. *Instead of seeing audio description as an opportunity to expand market share,*[2] these distributors may view it as a chore, a hassle, an added expense that takes resources away from other, more exciting areas. So, they don't invest much in it. They may even see that lack of investment, *or try to spin it* as a win for audiences: "My streaming service saves money by paying less for the AD it provides, so we can do more AD for you!"

But decisions to slash costs affects audiences in many unintended and negative ways.

Consider the impact on audience experience when AD facilities pay their workers less, eliminate entire departments ("Do we really *need* quality control?"), or double/triple up on responsibilities, having one person work across several specialized areas. As you can imagine, employees are more likely to miss errors—and create new ones—as a consequence.

With pay rates going down, many AD facilities are losing talented professionals who deliver top-notch work. When those pros leave, inexperienced people are hired to fill their shoes. The results are amateur at best, painful at worst: Poor casting. Tone problems. Heavy breathing. Missed cues. Bumpy transitions. (See the chapter on engineering and quality control for other issues that can stem from meager investment in AD.)

When cost cutting becomes the focus, AD becomes a roulette wheel of quality: who, or what, are you going to get on your project? Will audiences miss out on needed description for essential scenes? Will the script misidentify characters? Will the AD performance sound as if it was recorded in a bathroom?

These things happen when *too many* costs are cut—or

---

2 In addition to our many AD audiences, they also have friends and family who watch with them. And AD is not just for blind people: people on the spectrum can get more information that visuals may not fully inform. Also, sighted people use to do other activities, like driving, or cooking — or just giving their eyes a rest from screens.

when projects become races to the finish. Sometimes AD professionals are given very little time to create and perform the audio description. On more than one job, I've been asked to record several hundred cues within five hours of receiving the script and video. For the prime-time release of a TV show, I was brought to the studio to record that same afternoon, hours before the premiere. And once I produced AD for a film where, at the last minute, we had to fix the pronunciation of a main character's name. It took a team of four of us working together to deliver the new recording hours before the client needed the new AD version. I don't even want to think about the mistakes we narrowly avoided.

When AD is done cheaply and quickly, quality is going to suffer, and so will audience experience. The people doing the work will become disengaged, too.

Challenge 3: So much of this stuff is the SAME

Speaking of "meh"...a lot of AD has a same-old quality, like the overprocessed bologna sandwiches I used to pack in my school lunches.

From the mid-2010s and onward, titles for film and TV with AD exploded in number, from several dozen to over ten thousand.[3] As AD work has scaled, it's also been streamlined. That streamlining has a lot of benefits, like reducing duplicated effort and reaching more people with more titles. But a major downside to having set ways of doing things is that the workflow becomes a work trough: Flexibility and new approaches are shunned, because sameness speeds things up. If it works, we tend not to mess with it. As we keep innovation at arm's length, we fail to improve our processes, and we miss creative opportunities to meet audiences where they are.

---

3 https://adp.acb.org/masterad.html

Effective AD isn't one-size-fits-all. While standardizing processes increases efficiency and productivity, it's important to leave room for trying new things, too. Each film or show has its own story to tell. AD audiences have a spectrum of needs and tastes. Forcing audio description into the same tidy, rigid box each time you produce it makes for a bland audience experience. That's *not* entertainment.

Challenge 4: Audiences are forced to sacrifice quality for quantity

Studios and streaming services may try to convince themselves and their audiences that cost-cutting and streamlining will increase access. But a crank-it-out, more-is-more approach realistically leads to a substandard product: While there's more AD available, the quality can't possibly match what blind audiences know sighted audiences are getting.

Pitting quantity against quality unfairly blends two separate issues. It's discriminatory to put blind people in the position of giving up "better" for the sake of "more."[4] With the multitudes of high budget series and features, sighted people aren't expected to make that same tradeoff.

———

The four challenges above are just some of the problems that leave AD audiences feeling disconnected from shows and films. The end result is a degraded entertainment experience—certainly not what most directors and producers intend.

Some in the industry might suggest that AD audiences simply need to speak up about these obstacles to more immersive experiences. But why should AD audiences take responsibility for removing the roadblocks? We don't ask sighted audiences

---

4 It's bad business, too.

to do anything like that. And how should people "speak up," anyway? By calling customer service? Writing strongly worded emails? Sharing their frustrations on social media? Talking to theater managers? They've tried all that. Repeatedly.

Blind AD professionals shouldn't be expected to lead the charge, either. They're already quite busy doing their jobs. It's not their role to find and address all obstacles to accessibility. Forcing them into that position tasks them with the extra—and sometimes unwelcome—work of modeling what to do in an ideal world. (In the words of Chad Allen, a blind magician, interactive game consultant, and creator of the audio comic "Unseen": "I don't want to be a pioneer.") It puts their work under a microscope as they're trying to grow in their own careers.

That said, professionalism from *all* contributors, not just blind ones, is more than fair to expect and it has a big impact. Whether we're talking about performers, writers, editors, mixers, QCers, or directing and casting professionals, being the weakest link makes for a lesser AD experience.[5]

We can all strive to do things better for our AD audiences. Now let's look at how.

Professionalism Respects the AD Audience

To address challenges such as the ones outlined above, it will take a shared commitment—across AD departments—to raising standards and approaching this work with greater empathy for our audiences. Their needs should always be front and center. That's professionalism. And it's the road to parity.

Professionalism can be such an ethereal term! In the con-

---

5 See appendix, "The Weakest Link."

text of this book, I'm referring to the artistry, attitudes, ethics, intentions, and responsibilities, which lead to respect and accountability among peers — all to merit excellence in collaborations.

We can improve the audience experience by providing better audio.

Professional AD maintains the quality of the audio from the original production. If the production has Dolby Atmos, or surround sound, the AD gets the same treatment.[6] The overall sound experience is not degraded by a tacked-on extra track that's "not like the others." Each track supports and feeds the vision of the film. AD aligns with that vision of the film; it's no different than other approaches to better audio.

We can improve access with well-timed AD releases

Sighted and blind audiences should gain access to entertainment content at the same time. To that end, we can create audio description within the regular production process (rather than separately, in the distribution phase) and release the AD with the film or show.

I recently worked on a feature film with fully integrated AD. That means it's actually part of the movie for all audiences— not relegated to a track that's played only in certain versions or on special headsets. The basic idea was to shrink the gap between sighted and blind audiences so they could enjoy the experience together. We even incorporated a few jokes within the AD that support the story. This was such an exciting project, unique in its approach. Integrated AD ("open AD"—the audio description that is baked in) isn't the best solution for all entertainment media, yet I hope there are many more like it.

---

6 Apple TV+ titles have made this a standard for their originals.

We can make AD easier to find and customize

If we automatically turn on audio description in default settings, those who want it won't have to hunt for it, and others can simply turn it off. This approach isn't uncommon with closed captioning and enhancements like Dolby Atmos and Vision. Why not extend it to AD? The convenience of having it all up and running, like any other premium feature, allows audiences to personalize access to meet their particular needs.[7]

We can also give AD audiences access to who's worked on what

Before a film or show comes out, we can let audiences know which AD performers and writers they'll get. People who regularly use audio description have their favorite pros. They should have the chance to "opt out" if they don't like the AD lineup, just as they might if they didn't care for one of the actors, for instance, or the director or screenwriter. Knowing ahead of time who worked on the film makes an impact on audiences at large. Reputations of AD professionals—and AD facilities—also has an impact on our AD audiences.

We can make inclusion a priority

Thanks in no small part to public comments on the *Reid My Mind* podcast (which explores topics related to blindness and disability), AD facilities have been taking steps to make appropriate hiring decisions that align with the entertainment content. One of the biggest changes they've made, with potentially the greatest impact, is understanding the collaboration of disabled professionals—hiring AD performers and other professionals on the blindness spectrum—to the

---

7 Yes, I am making the argument that "accessibility" is an enriching feature - and AD audiences experience of an immersive story is a form of accessibility.

AD teams. Here's Satauna Howery, a voiceover artist who understands firsthand what it's like to rely on poorly cast AD:

> I was born blind. I don't have any sight at all. And, so, I am an audio description narrator but also a consumer of audio description. Which means I'm pretty opinionated about it, too...

> [I watched a few episodes of a show on] Netflix. The woman they cast to describe was, like, a grandmother who wouldn't know what was up for a 16-year-old if it conked her on the head. That's how I felt when I listened to her... And it was not that she did a bad job of performing it [at] all. It was just that she was the wrong person to be doing it.[8]

Efforts to increase inclusion in AD work are still in their infancy, and many shows still struggle to make appropriate hiring choices. Why? When projects are rushed by distribution or when facilities lack resources—both common issues—decision makers are less likely to spend time seeking out AD pros from marginalized groups, such as those with disabilities, people of color, and LGBTQ+ professionals. Instead, they bring in talent that's easy to find and schedule, which may lead to the wrong "fit" and limits opportunities for others to work, learn, and advance in their careers.

When inclusion is prioritized, however, studios and facilities gain access to a much wider world of talent and increase their odds of finding AD performers, writers, and quality control pros who are a more logical fit for their projects. That makes a significant difference in creating an immersive experience for AD audiences.

---

8 https://www.roysamuelson.com/interviews/satauna-howery/ and https://www.roysamuelson.com/interviews/satauna-voices-seinfeld/

This kind of intersectionality requires an extra layer of consideration, but the rewards are great and worth pursuing.

All this adds up to creating and delivering a professional product.

In short, AD that's professionally produced—at every step of the process—makes it equally easy for blind and sighted audiences to access and enjoy great movies and shows. It allows us to provide more and more emotional, nuanced, and immersive experiences to people who often don't get them in their entertainment—which means we'll eventually, if we keep at it, normalize these experiences.

Everyone, blind or sighted, will simply come to expect them, as well they should.

)))

CHAPTER 2
Bringing Your "A" Game to AD Performance

Bob Bergen is a four-time Emmy-nominated voice actor, best known as the voice of Porky Pig for Warner Bros. He's a member of the Television Academy and the Academy of Motion Picture Arts and Sciences, and one of the most in-demand voiceover coaches in the industry. When I corresponded with him recently, he had this to say about audio description:

> You're a performer, because you have to shift performance gears based on the genre. Perhaps based on the episode, perhaps within the episode, just like an on-camera actor does.

It's an important point—AD is a craft. It should be performed, not just read. But I'd like to clarify one thing: in this context, performing doesn't mean standing out. You have to strike a careful balance between channeling the emotional energy of the story—all the ups and downs—and blending in, so as not to distract. As AD aficionado Hannah Waymouth put it when we spoke:

> People who perform AD always say, "You shouldn't notice me. You shouldn't notice my voice. I should blend in the background." And at first I noticed it because I was not used to it. But then, I didn't notice it anymore. And it was just telling me everything. And now I completely agree... When you notice [AD performers] too much, it goes back to being a little jarring.[1]

How you say the words makes a difference. If an AD voice sounds bored, condescending, dull, chirpy, or otherwise "off," it essentially kicks the audience out of the immersive experience they're meant to have. People may also assume, quite fairly:

- It's not a real person.
- It's not a real performer.
- It's someone who's a real performer who's being directed by someone who's not a real director.
- It's someone who doesn't have access to resources to help them perform better.
- It's someone who's being directed by someone who's being hired by someone who doesn't care.
- It's someone who's being directed by someone who's being hired by someone who wants to train the audience to accept mediocrity.

Doing this job effectively (hitting all the right notes, but in an unobtrusive way) takes lots of technical skill and training. Does that mean AD performers are technicians rather than

---

1   https://www.roysamuelson.com/interviews/hannah-waymouth/

artists?

Well, they're both. Like practitioners of any trade—think plumbers, electricians, carpenters—they're trained to use specialized techniques *and* creative problem-solving to sort out, and meet, the particular requirements of each job. Clients may assume the work is straightforward and predictable, but that tends not to be the case.

To illustrate, let's pretend you're a plumber. Before entering a customer's home, you're typically asked, "How much will you charge?" At this point, however, you don't yet know what you'll repair. What's causing that flood in the basement? A broken sump pump downstairs? A leaky dishwasher or bathtub upstairs? Until you've rolled up your sleeves, it's impossible to identify the source of the problem, estimate how long it'll take to fix, and sort out whether you'll need to make a special run to pick up extra parts or equipment. So, based on your expertise and experience, you quote a flat rate for showing up and promise an estimate once you've done some diagnostics.

But when you arrive, the customer says you can't open any walls. Not only do you lack information about the problem—they are actively resisting sharing that information with you.

Also, they'll need you to finish up by 4 pm.

With a sigh, you do what you can and leave.

That's often what it's like for voice-over actors, including AD performers. They do their best considering whatever constraints they encounter. Frequently, they're asked for an up-front quote when the work to be done is very much an open question. When they do their job, they rely on most if not all their own gear (mics, pre-amps, and software are their versions of pipe wrenches, pliers, and plungers), along with their knowledge, ingenuity, and appetite for problem solving.

Instead of towels and drop cloths, AD performers use their technical prowess, research, and advisor tips to choose the best treatments (like bass traps, acoustic foam, and sound-dampening chambers) to filter out fan noise, to acoustically treat their recording spaces, and to remove echoes and ambient noises from neighbor's dogs barking or leaf blowers or helicopters. When they perform, they draw upon skills they've honed over years of training, coaching, and working in the field.

Unfortunately, many clients don't grasp the level of investment, skill, and creativity that goes into a professional AD performance. That can create the following challenges for performers, making it harder to maintain high quality standards.

Challenge 1: You're brought in to "just do it" as written

It's tough to perform audio description effectively if all you have to go on is what's written in the AD script. Production audio and video tracks provide a wealth of additional insight.[2] However, some AD clients don't offer access to those. Without that rich context, AD performers may (understandably) water down their reads so they're less likely to distract audiences from the rest of the production. But bland audio description can be distracting, too, because it doesn't blend into the rest of the entertainment experience.

Even if you make super-smart educated guesses about tone and intent based on what's in your AD script, your audio description may still sound lifeless or "off" when added to the final mix. That means your AD audience might wind up in the discriminatory position of enduring yet another amateurish read, despite your best professional efforts.

Let's look at how performances suffer when they lack access to two sets of context clues in particular.

---

2 A blind AD performer also needs access to the visuals. By adding "notes" to the script (essentially, describing what's on screen for the performer's benefit), AD writers can make this accommodation.

First, there's the **music**, which, in TV and film, has a powerful effect on the audience's emotions. Sadly, AD performers might not get access to this layer of audio when they do their reads, and so they miss opportunities to add nuance to the description.

A movie or show's score evokes an overall sense of foreboding, silliness, catastrophe, snarkiness, what have you. And within the story, the music reflects changes in emotional tone from scene to scene and even from moment to moment. Intensity may rise and fall and rise again. A character may express anger, then fear, then desire. With a little help from the music, the AD performer can swiftly roll with those tone changes.

I worked on a sci-fi series that, overall, had high stakes and tension. The opening scene of one episode showed a character walking around the set, interacting with various other characters. But the music was playful and gently sweet. Because I had access to that emotional shift, I put a smile on my face and followed the music's lead. Without the music, I would have read the audio description to match the general tone of the show: suspenseful, with an "Oh, no, what's gonna happen next?" subtext. Like many AD performers, I would have had to guess at what was happening with the emotional arc.[3]

Second, there's the **character dialogue** before and after each AD cue. As with the music, it's often absent from the AD script. Your script might say that two characters are slapping each other, for example—but without the surrounding dialogue, those slaps are subject to misinterpretation. You might read them as playful when they're meant to be violent. Or vice

3 Although it's widely accepted that AD writers need access to production audio and video, studios might not extend that same courtesy to AD performers. It's not clear why. Some inscrutable mix of legal and IP restrictions may be to blame. Whatever the reason, it seems narrow-minded to me. Performers are left doing a fair amount of guesswork, which just hurts the final product. It can be especially difficult for blind performers to piece things together.

versa.

AD audiences will notice that sort of emotional disconnect. If you can't fully tap into the story behind, or adjacent to, the audio description, you're just reading words. Performing AD with intention—infusing the words with relevant meaning—is what distinguishes immersive, memorable experiences from experiences that audiences will (or would rather) forget.

Music and character dialogue are such useful context clues because they shed light on emotional intent. AD performers who lack access to them may deliver every descriptive line the same way. Or they may channel the wrong emotions at inopportune moments. Either way, quality takes a hit.[4]

Quality can quickly go from iffy to downright bad if the edits are sloppy, because poor editing *obscures* emotional intent. It's another source of distraction that disrupts the audiences' experience.

As AD performer Satauna Howery put it when we spoke:

> We don't have a lot of control over how the final product is mixed. Some companies do that really well and some don't. Some just seem to duck the audio and you're either bowled over by the describer or, if the show gets really loud, then the describer gets really quiet. And that kind of mixing can take one out of the story, right? Because then I'm struggling to hear, or I'm hearing too much of the narrator.

In those ways, even an AD performer who somehow manages to "just do it" reasonably well, *despite* having limited access to emotional context clues, can easily be run off the rails in production.

---

4 Such problems tend to multiply when description is rendered by an AI voice or an unskilled performer. See appendix, "Text To Speech."

Challenge 2: You're thwarted by studio rules and facility logistics

Entertainment companies have lots of quirky little rules to follow. Each of those rules may make sense from a business standpoint, but they can really muck with AD performance.

For instance, consider all those **legal "oh-no-you-don'ts"** that can throw wrenches into audio description.

Some studios won't permit proper names or brands within the AD: It's a tissue, not a Kleenex. An SUV, not a Jeep.

OK, fine.

But a luxury sedan with a round hood ornament, not a Mercedes-Benz?[5] A flying disc, not a Frisbee? That gets awkward—not to mention blah—fast. Brand recognition is a shortcut to meaning. Replacing brands with generic language not only dilutes audience experience but can also lead to misinterpretation. (Is that flying disc a toy or a UFO?) Even names of famous people and characters are sometimes off limits. The grandma wearing the Taylor Swift T-shirt—how are you going to capture *her* essence in the show you're AD'ing without mentioning Ms. Swift?

As an AD performer, you may also get tripped up by **slapdash logistics**, which are more common than you might expect. Chances are, for instance, you won't receive your script until the very last minute. (*Instead of* hurry-up-and-wait, it's usually wait-and-hurry-up.) Ice-cold reads require certain skills to pull off, like understanding what makes AD writing effective and analyzing your cues on the spot. Remember, you might not get access to much else (see Challenge 1). If the AD writing is substandard, particularly with lots of unnecessary phrases, you'll have to quickly pick through it for insight, giv-

---

5 I am not a lawyer, but I understand the idea of protecting trademarks and copyrights, particularly if there's no license to use the word. I would want protections! Yet, the sighted audience can have the knowledge based on that very visual logo, or item. I wonder why, once that visual becomes a word, it's off limits?

en what you *do* know about the client and the project.

You also may have to jump through some **hierarchical hoops**, as well. Of course, performers should take direction graciously. But when direction is filtered through a third party, sometimes it's off target. You may have a strong hunch you should be reading your cues differently—but you have limited information, after all, and it's not your call anyway. So, you read those unnecessary filler words. You ramp up the animation, as you're asked to do, although you think the scene calls for a softer touch. And your heart sinks a little.

Facilities can also present some **technical hurdles**. They all seem to have their own processes and preferences that AD performers adapt to on the fly, with little to no preparation.

Some companies provide a streaming app that guides you from cue to cue as you record the audio description. Sessions like this are essentially "self-directed," aside from any special liner notes explaining that capitalized words are for EMPHASIS.

Other facilities provide a standalone AD script, along with video and audio from production, and you record the audio description after familiarizing yourself with the content. You get more information this way, but you're again mostly on your own in terms of direction.

Still other facilities schedule a remote session where you record from your own studio, using your own equipment and software. You just jump on a conference call and are told what to say. So, although you receive direction, it's in tiny, disconnected bits and pieces.

Whether you're recording at the AD facility's studio or at home, you'll probably encounter some hiccups. At the studio, the engineer or the director might have another urgent situation to address, causing delays to your scheduled session. At home, maybe the project's website locks you out hours before your AD recording is finished. Or maybe you've made some wrong guesses about context—and now you must redo all cues related to that one decision.

There's no shortage of technical and process challenges for AD performers to solve.

Challenge 3: You don't "belong" to the production

AD performers are usually hired by an AD facility, not directly by the show or film's production group. As a result, they may feel like outsiders, bouncing from project to project, isolated from the "core" team on each job.

It doesn't have to be that way.

Consider, for instance, how "loop groups" operate. These are voice actors who fill in background human sounds (say, in a coffee shop on set) after a film or show finishes shooting. Loopers enhance the audio atmosphere.

When I do this type of work (sometimes called ADR, or Automated Dialogue Replacement), I'm hired by production to record lines at a studio,[6] usually a postproduction sound stage, similar to what a movie theater would look like with all the seats removed. There's a microphone stand in front of the movie screen, and the voice actors walk in circles or shout from side to side or gather and talk, and the engineer records it. I shout, laugh, giggle, talk nonsense, or improvise lines of dialogue to match what's happening on screen. And when I'm done, the production compensates me according to the contract negotiated by my union.

As a looper, I'm usually paid the union's minimum wage[7]—a living wage that takes training and audition time into account as well as hours spent in the studio. Once I hit the annual income requirement, I qualify for my union's health coverage.

---

6 Historically, an actual location; some loopers now work remotely.

7 For a special voice that goes through an agent, it's minimum wage (scale) plus 10%.

This established way of doing business has worked for decades. I'm part of the regular production process, so I'm in the thick of it. I get all the information I need in order to do my best voice work.

Now, compare this with how most AD performers work. Somehow, in audio description many years ago, that model of the "production owning its content" was deconstructed. Union TV shows and movies would use AD performers like me, but the AD facility hired me to do the recording, so I was separated from the production process.

That has caused headaches for pretty much every department involved. More on that later. For now, it's important to know that AD performance often suffers as a result. The more isolated you are from core production processes, the less insight you have into the story that's being told, the characters who are telling it, and the experience the audience is supposed to have.

Challenge 4: Your calendar is filled with juggling & plate-spinning

Each AD facility has its own needs, approaches, and delivery requirements. As we discussed earlier, some companies share their AD script and production video/audio at the last minute, requiring a rushed performance. Others have more involved AD scripts (think action movies) with hundreds of cues. The quantity of lines to read and the amount of time it takes to record can vary substantially.

So how can you accurately gauge your availability to do the next gig and the one after that? It's not easy.

Complicating matters further, you probably won't have complete control over your own scheduling. When facilities give clients estimates of how long sessions should take, they're making reasonable guesses based on what they know about the projects. But sessions often end earlier or run later than expected. Leaving early might be a pleasant surprise if you could use a free afternoon. Or it might be annoying, because you've turned away other work that you *could* have done in that window. Of course, running late causes pileups.

Being at the end of the editing process leaves very little wiggle room in the AD performer's calendar. If a writer misses a deadline, that means you—and the engineering and quality control departments—have less time to do your work. You'll have to adapt to all kinds of changes and disruptions like this, at a moment's notice.

Unforeseen challenges in the work itself can derail your schedule, too. If unique word pronunciations aren't provided (or are provided in a way that requires even more research and guesses), you can wind up doing hours more work than anticipated.

When someone (like a QC specialist or an audio engineer) catches mistakes, the performer needs to record pickups so the AD facility can deliver a corrected track; if it's urgent and the performer isn't available, that can affect future work. The AD performer is effectively "on call" without necessarily being hired for those pickups, which crowds out opportunities to pursue other career or life activities. That's a common challenge for gig workers like AD performers, who are often cobbling jobs together to make ends meet.

Sometimes, an AD writer rewrites a script after listening to the recording. Some of the lines may make more sense, but substantial script rewrites can make a pickup session run much longer than the original recording.

Directed sessions involve more X factors: Was the AD script really a first draft, not edited prior to the session, and the director is editing on the fly during the session? Does the AD director have only surface familiarity with the content, because she's working on multiple other projects and there's no time? Are there delays with other projects, or business emergencies, or technical obstacles that could throw the session off schedule? As an AD performer, you can't always prepare for variables like these.

You have to try to impose some order in your calendar, though, or you'll lose it. Let's say you set aside a week for a client who needs multiple sessions. But then that client gets caught up in changes and delays that they didn't anticipate, which pushes your work further and further into the week that was set aside. At the end of that week, you look back and see a schedule clear of any commitments, but it's too late to fill it. That week was held for one client and lost to numerous others. The opposite can also happen: You've filled most of that time, and then your beleaguered client comes through after all. So now your work is rushed or otherwise compromised. Either way, it's tough to set aside time for anything else, like your family or your health.

(Isn't all of this exhaustingly disappointing? Please, keep with me, we've already offered some solutions, and there will be more.)

Challenge 5: Pay is a moving target

Compensation for AD performance is all over the place. For starters, rates vary by facility. Some companies pay a consistent amount from job to job; others adjust based on project length, project type, or hours in studio.[8] What's more, rates are watered down because competing AD facilities are looking to win clients by cutting costs. Performers' wages often don't reflect the value of their contributions. Sadly, some workers aren't even paid the agreed-upon rate for the

---

8 With hourly studio rates, performers who take longer make more money. While that can reflect an investment in quality, more often it creates an unintended consequence: inefficient beginners are rewarded financially for knowing less than pros who could do a better job in half the time.

job they've done.[9]

For these reasons—and to protect your self-worth, which is maybe the most important reason—you'll need to decide what's the lowest payment you would accept for each job and then *respect that boundary*. Without an industry-wide minimum payment, you're constantly negotiating—and if you sell yourself short, thinking it'll bring more work your way, you could end up getting paid substantially less than your colleagues for years to come. It happens. A lot.

Even if you're a crackerjack negotiator, though, you probably can't live off AD work alone. That's why so many seasoned voiceover pros are heading for the hills and making their living elsewhere, and cheaper amateurs are replacing them, lowering expectations all around for both pay *and* quality.

Compensation can be so low that some performers treat AD as a way of "giving back," practically (or literally) volunteering their time—which has the unintended effect of lowering average rates even more.

Performers may also accept almost nothing just for the privilege of associating with a high-profile project. If you're new to the business, your credibility goes through the roof when you're working on a well-known show. That credit is currency—and it's worth a lot. Trust me: I'm very familiar with the pull of "Oh, but wow, this credit would mean so much, I'll do anything to hang on." It's strong.

Challenge 6: There's room at the table, but no seats, for blind performers

---

9 Decision makers in fly-by-night facilities who don't fully understand the AD process might overpromise or underbill their client. Additionally, AD performers sometimes struggle for months or years to secure their compensation from companies that simply, and inexplicably, didn't pay them after services were rendered.

The challenges above can be especially daunting for AD performers on the blindness spectrum. Obstacles to information, to opportunities, to fair pay—they loom even larger if you already lack equitable access to the visual content you're meant to describe. Even when AD facilities and their clients want to adopt inclusive hiring practices and know it would be good for business, implicit biases often get in the way. That means blind AD performers must continually anticipate and counter those biases to get good work and build a solid track record in the industry.

As voice actor Tanja Milojevic points out:

> [You say to yourself], let's either not disclose to them because I don't want them to know, or let me try to make them feel as comfortable as possible... It's a slower process of building rapport in some cases, which can be a little intimidating.[10]

It can also be exhausting. While blind performers may be accommodated (or make their own accommodations) on any given project, fighting the assumptions of sighted people adds extra work.

Blind performers tell me they frequently educate their colleagues about their access needs. Sighted people unfamiliar with screen readers, for instance, might not understand why a blind person would be "looking down" at their phone. They might not consider that maybe this person is just listening or is able to see a little bit.

Blind performers also have to remind clients—again and again, it seems—that they know firsthand what works for AD audiences and what doesn't. Because they rely on audio description in their own lives, they bring a high level of commitment and dedication to this work. And still, clients who under-

---

10 https://www.roysamuelson.com/interviews/tanja-milojevic/

stand that in theory struggle to follow through in practice, for the same reasons they fail to invest in higher-quality AD more generally: The focus on cost-cutting in a competitive industry. The separation of AD from the rest of production. The relentless time crunch at the very end of the editing process.[11]

Challenge 7: You're caught up in needless professional rivalry

I've received phone calls from fellow AD performers asking why my voice, and not theirs, is on the final version of a project. But I myself have been replaced countless times on all kinds of projects—sometimes on one streaming service, sometimes on more. Once, I performed a whole season of a series for two different AD companies, and a third company also had its own AD version available.

I don't take it personally. And I don't see others' opportunities as my losses. AD work is not a zero-sum game. Remember, as of this writing, more than 10,000 films and series are listed as having AD on the Audio Description Project. That number will keep growing and growing.

We needn't worry about losing jobs to one another. We can all support each other and help each other learn and develop as performers. There's enough work out there for all of us, sighted and blind, so long as we are equally committed to delivering professional AD of the highest quality.

---

11 During Rebecca Odum's sensitivity pass, she had this comment to add: "It's also the fast turnaround that makes blind QC impossible to be part of the workflow. More time would make the overall quality much better. More time for the writers to write a well written script, more time for performers, more time for mix and QC. My hope is that QC will become part of the workflow and not just a few projects. QC is so important; as a consumer, I've heard so many AD tracks that had so many mistakes and could have been amazing with a QC pass."

It's Not ALL Bungled. Remember, We're *Pros*

That's a lot of challenges. And they come from all sides, often stemming from lack of awareness in the entertainment industry about what AD performers actually do for audiences.

Feeling a little overwhelmed? Yes? Then this is a great time for some "Serenity Prayer" vibes. While many things are outside our control, we can take meaningful steps to professionalize what we do day-to-day as individual performers—and in those small, iterative ways, we can create more immersive audience experiences.

Use your voiceover skills to their fullest

If you're a voiceover artist (even one new to audio description), you've acquired and fine-tuned many of the skills you'll need to bring AD audiences into the story being told. You can open the door to the experience a bit wider and invite people to come in and stay a while.

In a recent interview, my wonderful AD colleague Melody Goodspeed and I shared some thoughts on this topic.

> **Melody:**
>
> I want to use those inflections, those words, those colorful words, to bring the audience in, to lean into what's being said. And that's so important. It's important to lean into comfort. It's important to lean into something that really grabs you. You're passionate about it. You know, we take that stuff for granted. It's just nice to be able to close your eyes and then lean into a movie and just be confident and relaxed.
>
> **Roy:**

When I hear "lean in," I think "engagement": there's a connection there. That engagement, that connection, is a part of the big picture, so that [audiences] can feel like part of the conversation.

Melody:

It strengthens the relationship between the audience and the story.[12]

AD advocate Renee VanAusdall makes a similar point about that audience-story relationship:

If you've got somebody with a really good horror voice, and they...can create a mood...that doesn't break you away, then you have a deeper connection to what's going on. That narrator has an important job [to put people] in the right frame of mind so that they can stay with it and they can have what they need to decide how they feel about what's going on on-screen. There is nuance there.[13]

Mood, connection, frame of mind, feeling, nuance—this is the stuff of *all* great voiceover work. Whether they realize it or not, VO artists have been in training for AD performance throughout their careers.

Envision an ideal experience for the AD performer – and do what you can to lean into it

As we've discussed, there are limits to what we can control about our work environment. Some AD facilities bring performers into a physical studio to record; others collaborate

---

12 https://www.roysamuelson.com/interviews/melody-goodspeed/

13 https://www.roysamuelson.com/interviews/renee-vanausdall/

remotely. Some sessions are directed; others, less so. But whatever constraints you're given, you do have some room within them to shape your experience as a performer. Let's think for a minute about how that experience might ideally look and feel.

Most AD performance is done remotely these days. So, we'll start by imagining a video call where the director is at the facility (or maybe at home) and you're in your own recording studio far away. Once you each make some adjustments so that what you're hearing on both sides is in sync, you get started.

In an ideal world, you'll have already reviewed production audio and video from the show, along with your cues, your lines within them, and the timecodes that signal when you'll jump in and out. You've pulled all that together in advance so you could ask the director any questions up front, but everything is clearly spelled out.

Sometimes you just deliver the AD lines one after another, and AI[14] will pop them in where needed. But for this hypothetical project, you're pleased that you'll be reading lines exactly where they should go between bits of dialogue. This gives you much more control over your performance; it allows you to strike just the right tone and play with the intensity and pacing.

You're also happy to have the show's entire script available digitally, including the characters' dialogue, with your timecodes, lines, and cue lengths indicated throughout. You've found that having everything integrated into one file helps you perform better. Pauses are literally indicated with the word "pause." Scene changes are clearly flagged. Parentheses and capital letters are used to clarify word pronunciation and syllable emphasis.

---

14 Some AD companies have performers use software that does much of the syncing for them and protects the content from piracy risk.

The director, who's already familiar with the content and who knows how to pronounce all character names and unique proper nouns, guides the session. The engineer places each cue as you record it. This way, you don't have to deal with script changes on the fly, as often happens when an entire film or TV show session is recorded in real time. You also make fewer mistakes. And when you do make them, the engineer pauses the recording, takes it back maybe three seconds,[15] and has you rerecord that particular cue as a "pick up." Those few extra moments allow you a little lead time to ramp up your performance.

Since this session is remote, you are paid not only for the hours you spend recording but also for the use of your home studio to cover the investments you've made in procuring your own equipment and learning how to use it.[16] Any problems in the AD writing (wrong character names, script rewrites with the seams showing, dropped cues, missing guides for unique pronunciation) aren't your responsibility. You've agreed in advance that you'll be paid extra for any additional pickup sessions that might be needed.

Prior to the show's release, since AD audiences often like to know in advance who worked on the audio description, your performance will be noted on social media, on IMDb, and on the ADNA website.[17] And you'll be listed (along with the other pros who worked on AD, like the writer and the engineer) in the AD track's opening audio credits.

---

15 Engineers may use longer or shorter lead times, depending on how they prefer to work.

16 If you're recording from home without support from a director or an engineer, you should have at least two business days' turnaround time. For any less than that, I suggest charging a fee to expedite the recording, on top of your day rate and your home studio fee. Your time is valuable. In this working-solo scenario, any pickups to fix mistakes post-recording are your responsibility but should be given at least a day's turnaround time.

17 TheADNA.org provides a crowdsourced database of AD talents and their credits. It's basically the IMDb of AD.

That's how it's done when there's respect for this work.

Keep fine-tuning your craft

Like a play in a theater, AD that's professionally done can move an audience to tears by tapping into deep, heartfelt emotions. Or, in the hands of less-capable actors and writers, it can bring people to tears in another way: by making them so miserable that they can't wait to leave.

What distinguishes the pros from the hacks? Lots of practice, and a thoughtfully considered consensus on priorities.

Performers may regularly engage in voice workouts, for example. These are mock sessions or auditions where VO artists can get feedback and guidance without the pressure of having to "nail" a part. Voice workouts are incredibly helpful for keeping old skills sharp and developing new ones. You can experiment with new approaches and try out different types of reads. When you attend one of these, don't be afraid to stretch well beyond your comfort zone. This is your chance to grow.

Voice workouts used to mostly happen in a shared physical space, like a studio. But now many are done virtually, and so it's easier to bring people together. Virtual platforms do introduce some access challenges for blind performers, though, even when all participants are trained on the software. When planning a session, consider these potential hurdles—for instance, visual text that doesn't convert to Braille or a screen reader.

Practice makes professionalism. Pro athletes continue their training and coaching to stay on top of their game. So do pro AD performers. Otherwise, you get stuck in a formulaic rut of performing cues in the same way each time. Your lines come across as flat. Your work stagnates. There's no life to it.

Practice breathes life into performance. If you keep yourself in tiptop shape as a performer, you're better equipped to recognize the subtleties in each script, convey them, and put AD audiences in closer touch with what's happening on screen. The coaching and practicing should never stop. I'm frankly very leery of people who say that they have learned everything they need to know about voiceover or audio description.

I am constantly studying. There is always something new to learn or an old skill to reinforce. If you keep at it, the art of communicating emotional nuance through your VO and AD work will come much more naturally to you. Your skills will be honed and ready to kick in when you need them. It will become easier to deliver what each moment in the story calls for—and you'll be less likely to get in your own way by *overthinking* things.

One skill in particular that really helps actors and voice actors alike achieve this state of performance Zen is "playing the intention." We touched on this earlier, but it's so essential, in my view, that it merits more discussion. Immersive AD performers don't simply "say it happy" or "say it sad." Instead of just *indicating emotions*, they dig into the motivation behind each line so they can ride the emotional highs and lows and bring the audience along.

Intentions are action verbs. For example: *When I describe this scene, I want the audience **to cry**. Or **to cower**. Or **to cringe**.*

Many of my acting coaches insist on bringing this focus to character work, and I've found that it's equally powerful when applied to audio description. If you're an actor, your goal is to tap into your character's motivation. If you're an AD performer, your "character" is the voice that describes the visuals on screen.

Since stories are told, and characters are developed, in no small part *through* the visuals, it makes sense that the visuals, too, would be packed with intention. As an AD performer, you can surf these intentions to ride the story's emotional wave.

You're never too experienced to practice playing the intention. It's a basic skill, but it gets rusty if you don't keep using it.

Know where you can learn at every level

At each stage of your professional development, you'll find different ways to acquire and practice the skills you need. VO performers who are new to AD will start with the basics. To return to the sports analogy: you might think of this stage as "little league," where you'll get up to speed on the fundamentals.

One place where anyone can get free AD experience, right away, is on YouDescribe.org, a website where blind people can post YouTube videos and request audio description for them. You're volunteering here, and it's understood that you may be learning as you go. Try collaborating with a newbie writer to craft and perform AD scripts for one or more of these videos. You don't have to do everything! Choose projects that truly appeal to you. You'll put more energy into them and, as a result, learn more from them.

To connect with aspiring AD writers, try visiting the Audio Description Discussion Group on Facebook. By teaming up with someone who loves what you *don't* do, you can focus on developing your area of expertise, they can focus on developing theirs, and along the way you can both still learn a little more about each other's craft.

As you do more and more AD, you'll discover what works and what doesn't.

Another great skill builder is simply reading things out loud—books, magazine articles, even emails—to practice getting the words out of your mouth. Getting those speaking muscles aligned with how you read words in your mind is absolutely essential for AD performers. Since most AD readings are ice cold, you'll need to practice and practice this skill so it comes easily to you in the moment. Then you can stop trying so hard and start sounding more natural.

Once you've begun taking on professional AD assignments, you can think of yourself as a "junior varsity" performer. You've picked up considerable knowledge and gained confidence, but you're not yet a seasoned pro.

At this level, a terrific way to practice is to regularly help a group of writers when they workshop their plays, scripts, and other content by reading their material (including any stage directions) aloud for them. Remember, I did this weekly for *ten years*, and it helped me at least as much as it helped the writers. While offering your services like this is not the same as doing audio description, it cross-trains the "cold reading" muscle, which you'll use all the time as an AD performer.

To build other skills that can easily transfer to audio description, I highly recommend taking part in acting and voice-over workshops. AD performance is specialized work, but it's still a form of acting.

Eventually, as you hone and enhance your AD techniques, you'll move on to the "major leagues," but you'll continue to seek out opportunities to practice and learn. At this point in your career, you can also really lean into your AD network. You've been in the business long enough to have formed relationships with some real pros. You'll all benefit if you support and mentor one another—and advocate for one another.

As your experience deepens, you'll probably also find that you're digging more deeply into the content and the cues as you prep for your performances. For instance, when I receive an AD script, I comb through it for the tiniest details. I glance at the length of the cues. I check for a pronunciation guide. I look for any subtitles that I might have to do. If there are a lot, I might recommend that the facility assign those lines to one or more VO actors who specialize in dubbing.

The truly committed AD professional undertakes to do

more homework and prep work than clients might ever imagine. It's unpaid, but it pays off. If the show hasn't come out yet, I see if there's a trailer. Or I look at what else the director and screenwriter have done. I want to get a sense of flavor.

Although each line has an intention behind it, not everything is important. Some phrases or cues deserve more weight than others. I make note of which ones to emphasize in my script.

I note the importance of the nouns, too—the people, places, and things in the story—and switch up the emphasis accordingly. A beloved character coming back unexpectedly will get a lot of love in my cue. An unwelcome character might be met with a chillier intention, like "to disrespect" or "to disappoint." I leave enough space between my sentences to allow for some processing.

As I'm poring over a script, I can tell right away if the AD writer didn't read the words out loud—the pace is consistently brisk. When that's the case, I know I'll need to add speed without sacrificing intention or clarity. Once again, those cold-reading skills will come to the rescue.

There's a necessary counterpart to all this detailed prep: a willingness to just *go* with things. That might be the hardest skill to master as a performer. It goes hand-in-glove with being prepared, though. If you've got the nitty-gritty issues covered, that frees you up to respond authentically—and flexibly—to the emotional content of the story.

I like the way AD performer Laine Kelly describes this skill when we spoke:

> Yeah, you have to flex, right? Because if it's an action scene, you wanna be a little bit more high energy, have some more tension in your voice, maybe bring it down with a little bit more gravitas. But if it's a love scene, you are not gonna

sound like that 'cause you'll sound like a weirdo <laugh> or creeper. So yeah, you do kind of flex like you would in any conversation or whatever is going on in life. You'd flex depending on what's happening in front of you.[18]

If you're flexing effectively in your AD reads, you are an immersive performer—and a true pro.

Navigate the industry with grace and grit

Of course, there's more to professionalism than nailing each performance. It's also about how you participate in the AD community and the entertainment industry, as a whole.

You will come up against obstacles no matter how talented you are. For instance, even the most seasoned performers may struggle to land jobs they know they can do beautifully. The audition process for audio description varies by production company. Knowing how each company lines up talent will save you from bloodying your knuckles, knocking on all the wrong doors. Some want a very specific voice sound and, on that basis, make their casting choices almost instantly. Others have a pool of AD performers they trust to deliver again and again. Do your research so you know where it makes sense to go.

With so much new content coming out, audio description work is attracting scads of voiceover performers. To stand out, don't hesitate to list your non-AD credits to showcase your talent. These other VO experiences can be framed to highlight parallels to the AD jobs you're pursuing, and having many credits to your name shows *hireability.*

You might actually have greater leeway to list your non-AD work. Sometimes AD performers aren't permitted to share

---

18 https://www.roysamuelson.com/interviews/laine-kelly/

their credits publicly because the facilities they work for don't own the film or show. (They are facility contractors, and so the studios don't treat them as individual "creatives.") This puts performers in a bind, of course: how can they promote their experience and talent without sharing the details of the projects they've worked on? The facilities doing the hiring understand this constraint, though. They expect you to highlight non-AD jobs when you audition for AD work.

How else can you get in the door? Many performers cold-call AD facilities, on the hunt for random opportunities. This is neither efficient nor particularly effective. Others take a more strategic approach: they do their research to find out what companies are looking for and how they work with talent, follow up with appropriate messaging, and then attend auditions with their most relevant skills at the ready.

When coaching, I encourage performers to approach audio description facilities in ways that showcase their individuality. What sets them apart? A quirky voice? An ability to do several voices? Whatever it is, embrace it. I also strongly suggest gaining experience in voiceover acting and AD performance— through workshops, volunteer work, and so on—*before* approaching one of these facilities for a job. There's too much competition to do a trial-by-fire audition. Performers who clearly aren't prepared will quickly get screened out of current *and* future opportunities.

In most cases, auditions are done remotely, so having a home studio is very helpful. To learn how to set one up, visit IWantToBeAVoiceActor.com. I use this website regularly and find it incredibly valuable. It offers a wealth of information about all things VO.

If you ace the audition and get an offer, certainly savor that moment—but ask for the terms in writing before you take the job. Countless agreements specify a dollar rate without detailing the workload, deliverables, timing, expectations, or use.

Will your recording be used in a nationally broadcast commercial? Will it be fed into an AI system for future "tbd" projects (meaning you'll have no say in how your voice is used after it's recorded)? How many pickup rounds (for rerecording lines) are included in your rate? Will you need to record on a certain microphone or use a certain software? Will you have access to production audio and video?

Having all the details spelled out in your contract will help prevent misunderstandings and minimize frustration later. And keep drawing on the relationships in your network. By checking with others who have worked with the client—before you sign anything—you can avoid some dangerous waters. As a freelancer, you are the only entity invested in your professional security and success. Take that investment seriously.

Finally, whether you're sighted or blind, keep fighting the good fight for parity: Equal access to training and work. Equal status. Equal pay. Equal credit. We can support one another during practice sessions by providing feedback in a way that's easy for each individual to understand and apply. In doing so, we create inclusive opportunities for learning—and for getting jobs. Practice is a form of networking, after all. We shouldn't look at accessibility in professional development as going above and beyond. It should simply be a given. As for the work itself, we're still far from leveling the playing field. Anecdotally, I've learned that blind performers are sometimes paid half of what sighted performers make—and that is appalling.[19] When pay information is kept private, parity becomes harder to achieve.

Blind performers need not disclose their blindness in advance if they don't want to do so. That's up to each individu-

---

19 A few AD facilities are actively recruiting AD performers and QC specialists who are blind. But when competing against one another for projects, they may look for ways to trim costs and offer the prospective client a better deal, which brings wages down even further.

al. To be sure, being hired as "blind" talent adds complexity, thanks to non-disabled people's assumptions about blindness. During our interview, Satauna Howery described it as a "double-edged sword." She tends not to disclose her blindness before auditions, but she's open about it in her professional profile online. As she explained:

> I get to choose, and that provides a certain level of control. I can kind of control that shock-and-awe value. [But] every now and then, I'll get someone who will contact me, and they'll say, "Hey, you know, I Googled you. And I noticed that you're blind. Is there anything I can do to make this easier for you? What can I do?" And wow. That's exciting. So, it's a tough one. Like I said, I don't hide it. If you looked at my social media, if you Googled me, you would see it, but I don't directly state it.[20]

Some companies I've worked with have hired blind performers at my recommendation without knowing they are blind. I've also recommended performers explicitly because they are blind and because of their skillset. Both approaches can work, but whether to disclose a disability up front is definitely the performer's decision to make.

Facilities that hire blind talent come to recognize the benefits of inclusion. As composer Stephen Letnes put it in our interview, "hiring people with disabilities...simply broadens minds." He added:

> If you're patient enough and willing to ask questions and to be open to expanding your mind, [it] makes us better people... Maybe that's a super-Pollyannaish way to look at it. But that's how

---

20 https://www.roysamuelson.com/interviews/satauna-howery/

I wanna look at it.[21]

I love this outlook, and I wish everyone shared it. Unfortunately, good intentions don't always translate into good outcomes for performers. You do have to look out for your interests.

While we have a long way to go to reach parity, some blind AD performers are experiencing positive changes in the industry. In an interview, Ren Leach, a blind voiceover actor and AD performer, told me he's "starting to find that being blind is becoming less of a roadblock for narrators getting into the field." That's a big deal. So, what's the next step, once you're in? Leach adds: "I think that what I have to do is to continue to try as hard as I can to make the best possible project that I can."[22]

That commitment to making the best possible project makes *him* the best he can be. The same is true for all of us, whether or not we can see.

---

21 https://www.roysamuelson.com/interviews/stephen-letnes/
22 https://www.roysamuelson.com/interviews/ren-leach/

CHAPTER 3

Understanding the AD Writer's Lot

It's useful to know, as a performer and fellow accessibility champion, what goes into writing an effective AD script. Is it simply a matter of describing the visuals on screen?

Ummmm, no.

AD writing, like performing, is very much a craft. When audio description is really well crafted, it *subtly* helps move the story forward and emotionally immerse the audience in that story. The writing captures the feeling and intensity of each moment without drawing attention to itself or otherwise disrupting the story's flow.

To illustrate, here's a brief excerpt from an AD script that I think works well, from the TV series *Barry*:

> *Fuches sits in the middle of a back seat. His mouth gapes as he stares forward unblinking.*
>
> *A smaller silver car cuts through an intersection and speeds down the road. Barry sits at the*

wheel. He looks through the front windshield with an angry intensity.

In the Nohobal lobby, Hank steps in front of the statue of Cristobal. His men line up beside him, armed with automatic weapons. One of them ushers Sally in.

Hank stares at the lobby's front door. His expression softens as he watches Fuches slowly walk in with a large group of men carrying guns. They cross the lobby and stand before Hank and his men.

Holding eye contact with Fuches, Hank rests his hands on his hips.[1]

The action, the intensity, the range of emotions—it's all (quietly) there.

There's no exact formula for this stuff. AD writers make subjective choices all the time. They each use their own special blend of skills. The real pros work continually to overcome their particular areas of weakness.

Take David Strugar, an AD writer who initially struggled with brevity:

> You need to get the point across and get it across clearly in time to fit between lines of dialogue. And that really pushed me hard. The first few months...I was getting feedback constantly and just noticing how redundant and lazy, for lack of nicer words, my own writing was: "Oh, I need to cut back on that. I can stop using this phrase 'cause it doesn't actually do anything."[2]

1 AD written by James Mason, edited by Shane Weathers

2 https://www.roysamuelson.com/interviews/david-strugar/

He works hard to keep things tight. Other writers may focus more on controlling their tone, for instance, or perfecting their timing. These are all good things—prioritized in any number of ways, depending in part on the writer's idiosyncrasies and tastes.

Of course, audiences have their idiosyncrasies and tastes, too. Our friend Hannah Waymouth, the AD fan you met earlier, especially appreciates scripts that zero in on the most pertinent visuals:

> When I ask people to describe things, they have a hard time with it. A lot of people don't understand what is relevant. They don't know when to say something...It really is trying to figure out, where do you say things [and] how much do you say?[3]

So, in addition to being masters of timing, diction, and brevity, the best AD writers are curators *and* creators. They equip performers to say just enough, at just the right moments, in just the right words, to communicate the story behind the visuals.

That's why I believe it's misleading to call audio description "closed captioning for blind audiences." Unlike closed captioning, AD isn't an exact transcription. On the contrary, the writer chooses each word. In some ways, the work is similar to translating a book into a screenplay: Although it's based on existing source material, telling the story requires creativity and careful judgment about what to include and how to convey it.

It's a unique skillset, applied to a whole bunch of challenges; and we do better as performers and collaborators when we appreciate those skills and understand the obstacles AD

---

3 https://www.roysamuelson.com/interviews/hannah-waymouth/

writers face.

Let's Think About What Makes AD Writing HARD

Here are some of the thorniest challenges that AD writers must navigate.

Challenge 1: The writer can't (and shouldn't) describe it all

In AD, time's a-ticking. So, the writer must be decisive about what to omit. That's just as important as knowing what to include—maybe even more important, because leaving stuff out makes room for what matters.

This is about focusing on the visual details that best serve the story *and* making every word earn its keep. It takes considerable work and expertise to do both things well. So, as a performer, if you notice a few extraneous bits here and there in the AD script, just imagine how many *other* peripheral details have been surgically removed. As a result of the AD writer's smarts and sweat, you can deliver your lines with impact and the audience can process the description while also taking in the music, the dialogue, and all other things audio.

AD writers develop this skill over time. Beginners are often afraid to leave things out, which can lead to a less-than-immersive audience experience.

To make the point, here's a pretend sample:

> But then, suddenly—for a moment, while they are walking—the sun shines while waves lap and the couple kiss. They stare deeply into the distance and then furrow their brows.

Painful, right? The challenge isn't just (or even mainly) the purple prose—although the prose is, to quote Buddy the Elf, "very purpley." It's the descriptive clutter that's causing the

Hemingway in our hearts so much agita.

Let's deconstruct:

> "But" can easily be dropped. It's an unnecessary judgment. The writer doesn't have to explicitly signal a contrast between this moment and what happened before; the performer can do that vocally, with tone and pacing.

> "Then" can go, too. One thing happens. Another thing happens. That's life! In most AD situations, like this one, "then" is a redundancy. People won't get lost without it.

> "Suddenly" — let's drop these wasted syllables, as well, and see what can be accomplished in their absence.

> We can also cut "for a moment." Whatever follows this moment will inevitably be something new, and the performer can signal that shift with a brief pause.

> "While they are walking" kludges things up by combining unrelated events. At best, the added layer of explanation is confusing or distracting ("What's happening when? And how are these people walking and kissing at the same time? That takes balance!"). At worst, it sounds condescending, like "let me tell you step by step what this moment involves so you can follow it." The passive verb isn't doing us any favors, either. We can simply say, "They walk," and move on.

> The sun shining "while" the waves are lapping — again, tying these sequential-but-unrelated events together takes the audience out of the

story. People may get sidetracked wondering, consciously or not, "*Why* are we connecting these things?"

Staring "into the distance" implies "deeply." That's another redundancy.

"Furrow their brows" is a cliché in any type of writing—one that has actually become a joke among blind audiences, given how frequently it pops up in audio description. It can go.

Once we make those adjustments, what's left of our sample? Something like this:

> *On a remote beachside, the sun shines. (PAUSE FOR KISS) They stare toward the horizon.*

With fewer words describing the scene, there's now more room for the audible kiss, which can speak for itself. And the AD performer can be trusted to pick up on the furrowed brows and read the final line "they stare..." with the intent "to solemnly search" so the AD audience will sense the emotional longing.

The writer and the performer—and the rest of the team—need to work together to interpret the visuals in an accessible way.

Challenge 2: AD writing and other writing are different beasts

While many of the usual rules apply (strive for clarity, cut excess verbiage, etc.), AD writing also requires a specialized skillset. Not all singers are trained in opera. Most aren't. The same goes for writers and audio description.

They learn what works through mentoring, coaching, and

lots of practice.[4]

When we're in a newbie writer's hands, it's a different story. The script might omit punctuation cues, leave pronunciation of obscure proper nouns to the imagination, skip over important visuals, over describe unnecessary elements, or fill every silence with descriptive text. It might fail to clarify where critical sounds, like gunshots and car explosions, are coming from, and which characters are dying as a result. Or it might state the obvious. As Renee VanAusdall put it in our interview, "You know, of course, when a train comes into the station. It sounds like a train coming into the station!"[5]

I always like to say that if the proverbial picture is worth a thousand words, and a film or show has 24 pictures, or frames, per second,[6] every second is packed with 24,000 words' worth of information. That means the visuals in a 90-minute (or 5,400-second) movie *could*, in theory, be described in 130 million words.

There's *no good way* to cram in all that description. Even if it were possible to accommodate half that amount by plowing over lines of dialogue and other audio elements, that would ruin the audience experience.

True AD-writing pros focus relentlessly on audience experience. They do not indulge in any flourishes that could sabotage that goal.

If an AD performer has just a few seconds to read a cue, extraneous words will make the performer rush that cue. While AD delivery is often brisk by necessity, excessive speed overwhelms the audience with too much information at once, like a Cheesecake Factory menu, and leaves no room for

---

4 As performers, if we recognize and appreciate these AD writers' expertise when we see it, we can read our lines with greater confidence. It frees us up to focus on our craft.

5 https://www.roysamuelson.com/interviews/renee-vanausdall/

6 https://www.masterclass.com/articles/how-frame-rates-affect-film-and-video

nuance. *As we may by now know in AD, one enemy is "time."*[7]

Often, given time constraints, AD writers even omit *important* visuals—a character's eye roll, for example, done in response to another character's seemingly neutral statement—and trust the performer to convey intent. So, patience and good faith are essential tools in their kits. As performers, we can earn (and reinforce) their patience and good faith by vocally communicating those unscripted bits of context and emotional connection that move the story forward.

Challenge 3: Clients can make it tough for AD writers to do their jobs well

Like performers, when AD writers don't get all the information they need, they're left scrambling to fill in blanks on their own—for example, plot elements that seem insignificant early in a series but will resonate later. A heads-up about such things can prevent confusion and last-minute rewrites. Often, AD clients are so busy with other tasks that this sort of communication with the writer is rushed or doesn't occur at all. Or the opposite can happen. Some clients are so communicative that they micromanage the audio description process and even ask for things that the writer knows are not useful, like too much detail and flowery language that gilds the AD lily.

AD writers must manage a constant push-and-pull tension: If they bend to the client's will, how will that affect accessibility and audience experience? If they don't, will they lose this job or take themselves out of the running for the next one?

The short answer: The client is always right.[8]

---

7 I have been and remain a Cheesecake Factory fan. I just accommodate the visit with extra time for the page turning, and the decision overwhelm.

8 Even when the client is wrong.

BUT: When performers realize that the AD writer's back is against an unyielding wall, they can empathize. They can look for workarounds to minimize the effects of "forced errors" and improve accessibility. That extraneous line of description that production insisted on keeping? Maybe the performer creates space for it with some deft dialogue-dodging, and the audience's experience of that scene remains largely intact.

Sometimes compromises and sacrifices are needed to get the AD where it needs to be. There's no perfect solution. But solid communication between writers and performers on the facility side (and even the AD client's side!) can help make up for any disconnect between AD and the creative production.

Challenge 4: Writers get rushed—all the time

Impeccably polished AD scripts are rare, and the writers aren't to blame. Behind the scenes, they're expected to deliver against impossibly tight deadlines. Sometimes the budget for creating the AD is slashed and quality-assurance corners are cut as a result, which leads to extra rewrites with no extra time allotted. Sometimes the creative production is running way off schedule and so the AD script must be written and rewritten on the fly to hit the release date.

AD performers feel the crunch. I've been given scripts just hours before the show is released on streaming. But the writers tend to feel it even more—from all sides. In a day or less, they're asked to crank out many cues, placed perfectly between bits of dialogue. And then, as the creative script changes underfoot, they're frantically cutting and adapting as best they can.

When we acknowledge this reality as performers and flex with our writing colleagues, we can make the best of whatever circumstances are thrown our collective way. That isn't to say "the system" is just peachy as is. It's kind of messed up, thanks largely to the common relegation of AD work outside even postproduction and into distribution's hands. But that challenge isn't something that we performers and writers can solve among ourselves. We can push for change in the industry and, in the meantime, we treat one another collegially and bring as much professionalism to our work as possible, given the realities.

How Can We Create a Better World for AD Writers?

As Nathaniel Hawthorne once said, and Maya Angelou reminded us, "Easy reading is damn hard writing."[9]

In the AD world, this is doubly true. But if we could create a better world for AD writers, we'd make their "hard writing" a bit easier, and we'd all benefit. Just imagine: less harried writers would produce tighter AD scripts, leading to more nuanced performances and immersive audience experiences.

But what would that world look like?

Let's dream big for a minute, without limiting ourselves to what's currently within our control.

For starters, writers would have more information. They'd be fully briefed, early on, as to where the story is going. For example, in a series, they'd know the scope and arc of the season in advance so they could deftly signal to the audience where things are headed, without revealing too much. They'd receive access to the actual shooting script and notes about any special names, locations, and items unique to the story, particularly in science fiction shows or other stylized storytelling worlds.

Writers would also, in our AD paradise, get more time

---

9 https://www.theparisreview.org/interviews/2279/the-art-of-fiction-no-119-maya-angelou

to process all this valuable information. Just ask Christina Stevens, who has created AD scripts for a number of prominent series and films, how she likes to work:

> I watch the whole movie through once at least. And then I take lots of notes…[about] characters and plot points, and when things are introduced, and then I start writing. It is sort of a tedious process, as you can imagine. [But I'm] learning so much more about the story.
>
> Once I start writing, I'm picking up little things here and there. It's basically like watching a movie dozens of times, because I'm watching it that closely to try and fit in all the details and kind of get the feel of every scene and try to capture what the artistic intent is of everything. That's the process.
>
> Once I'm done with the first or rough draft, I'll read through the whole thing once more. You catch stuff at that point, just because you're trying to get a big picture and the little picture at the same time…
>
> *We're not like* casual movie watchers.[10]

A better world for AD writers would also include more training on how to meet audiences' accessibility needs. To keep their skills sharp, they would regularly attend retreats like those run by Colleen Connor, a blind theater actor who *knows* the AD industry and teaches writers about current trends and approaches—such as using inclusive they/them pronouns for individual characters and taking care to correctly identify culturally specific items on screen.

---

10 https://www.roysamuelson.com/interviews/christina-stevens/

Perhaps most important, this wonderful world would be enriched by collaboration and a sense of community. As isolating as AD writing can feel, it shouldn't be a solo job.

That's true for performing, too. We're in this together.

)))

CHAPTER 4

Making Life Easier for Friends who Fix Things in Engineering and QC

Sound engineers and quality control specialists are audio alchemists. They mix and fix the AD so it's not too loud or too soft, or tromping on lines of dialogue, or punctuated by distracting breaths or sneezes or chair squeaks or those neighborhood parking dogs.

These two departments remove all manner of oopsies that would get in the way of an immersive audience experience.

The Engineers Bring It All Together

Jeff Ross, an AD sound engineer, points out that all audio elements are surrounded by other audio elements and should be managed accordingly:

You really have to balance in audio description to

not overpower the content of the movie, which is a pretty easy thing to do. If you're not paying attention and you just set the fader at one level and let it ride through the whole movie, it's not going to result in the best product...

The music holds emotional content, [like] the dialogue of the movie. You want to leave room for that stuff to breathe and to be able to be heard under your narration.[1]

Without the benefit of sound engineering, the audience might have to keep fiddling with their volume controls to even hear the AD. Or they might suffer through 30 or 60 or 90 minutes (or more!) of obtrusive voiceover description that upstages everything else, like an old-time radio DJ talking over a song.

It's not all about volume, though. Jordan O'Neill, another sound engineer, expands on the department's responsibilities, which have evolved thanks to advances in technology and trends in remote work:

Most voiceover artists are recording from home. What happens on the other side of that track when a sound editor receives it? We'll remove any unnecessary silence between takes, pop snaps, or clicks that might be inherent, even at a minimal level in any kind of recorded track.

Then there's a little bit of [equalizing] and de-essing for the various voiceover artists, depending on where their voice registers, whether they have a deep voice or a high voice, whether there's a lot of tongue clicks going on when they speak. All of

---

1 https://www.roysamuelson.com/interviews/jeff-ross/

those nuances are something to keep in mind when [equalizing] certain frequencies in and out.

The de-essing that takes place for hard p's and b's and s's—you want to smooth those out so they aren't so present.

Depending on the content that that voiceover is going to be played against, you may need to boost the overall mixed levels. You may need to find kind of a middle ground.

Then, the mixing is usually concerned with the consistency of the performance of the voice-over artist and the print master audio and the dynamics of that content. So, whether it's a dialogue-driven show or an action-driven show will [affect] how you balance the voiceover artist against the periodic dipping of the print master, to allow for that AD voiceover track to be present in the mix.[2]

At the same time, you don't want to take away from the original mix's dynamics. You wanna find that balance.

When the audio mix is working as it should, you don't notice it. But when it's not, it sticks out in lots of ways, big and small. If the AD sound engineer isn't paying close attention to the story, for example, and a comedy moment comes too early or too late in the audio description track, AD audiences will laugh before or after everyone else. Or if the production audio ducks behind the AD performer for extended periods, people will likely miss key bits of dialogue and other important story elements.

Just one or two little glitches—audiences tend to forgive

2 https://www.roysamuelson.com/interviews/jordan-oneill/

those. They *want* to stay immersed in the moment. But they get really annoyed with shows and movies that are riddled with audio problems, even if they can't identify exactly why they're annoyed. For an audience member who also happens to be a sound pro, it's hard to think about anything *but* those problems. BeSharp Studio owner Slau Halatyn, a blind engineer and producer, shares this perspective:

> People ask me whether I can just sit and listen to music and appreciate it for what it is without analyzing it. And I must say it's difficult... I sit there and I wish they would've done this or that, or whatever it is. And it's pretty much the same with audio description. I mean, how could you not sit there and roll your eyes when something is suddenly ducked so far down that you hear the audio description clearly, but you hear none of the program material behind it? And then suddenly that program material shoots up again? It's very distracting, you know? So as a professional, I sit there and I listen, and I go, "oh, that's terrible."[3]

In the hands of a poorly trained engineer—or even a good one who is being rushed—the whole AD track might slide off by a few seconds, or individual cues might not align in between lines of dialogue. To compensate, the engineer might then speed up the AD performer's voice, chipmunk-style. You can imagine the cascading effects.

Avoiding such issues altogether, a clever sound engineer makes accessibility feel natural, not like an interactive game for blind people. What we're talking about here is continuity of experience. People in the audience should not have to work

---

3 https://www.roysamuelson.com/interviews/slau-halatyn/

hard to reconcile the AD with the rest of the audio.

Writer and director Brian Herskowitz recently wrote that sighted audiences "have an expectation that what they hear will match what they see."[4] I think blind audiences should expect similar alignment between the production audio and the AD.

QC Helps Us Fix Our Mistakes

If sound engineers stitch the various audio elements together in a cohesive way, it seems fair to say that the quality control folks smooth out those seams. But really, QC specialists support the contributions of all AD departments. They might step in at one or more stages to offer notes not just on audio issues but also on the AD script's accuracy and clarity, the performer's tone and approach, and the overall audience experience.

They are responsible for finding mistakes but must rely on the other departments to implement fixes (if there is enough time before the release deadline). Pronunciation errors and inconsistencies, run-on sentences, grammatical mistakes, misread lines, missed cues, audio glitches, and many more issues can come roaring into a project postproduction. As one of my editors put it, without a sharp set of QC eyes to catch them, all this "could be a hot mess."[5]

Many AD facilities are boosting accessibility by hiring QC specialists. Sadly, though, they're competing against companies that don't provide this much-needed service and that charge less as a result.

---

4 https://www.linkedin.com/advice/1/how-can-you-use-adr-maintain-continuity-between-vj35f
5 Thanks, V.

Quality control preserves the integrity of the AD. People who do this work well approach it with empathy, immersing themselves in all the details so their blind audiences, too, can feel immersed. That's how Juan Alcazar, a blind filmmaker and QC specialist, processes the content before sorting out what challenges need to be solved:

> When I'm doing QC for audio description, I kind of have to get lost in the content itself, to just recognize the context of what's happening on screen. But at the same time, as soon as I go through a second pass of that same line or cue, I have to disconnect myself and be like, "Okay, now, technically is everything fine here?" So it, it's almost like a constant tuning in and tuning out.
>
> My initial thoughts of QC were kinda like it was just someone making sure that everything sounds right, all the t's are crossed, i's are dotted, things like that. In a way it is, but at the same time it's more than that. Context-wise, does a line fit? Does this need to be rewritten in a certain way?
>
> ...I'm giving that last check before things are approved. It might be different from place to place, but definitely I see it as one of those very last steps. It's a very tight deadline, and it really depends on the timeframe that we're given to finish these projects. Sometimes, being detail oriented and on a tight deadline—those two things don't generally mix.[6]

As Alcazar suggests, quality control specialists in AD cov-

---

6 https://www.roysamuelson.com/interviews/juan-alcaza

er a lot of territory; like a script supervisor, they oversee the continuity, flag mistakes and ambiguities, note audio glitches, and so much more. They are also under super-tight deadlines, because QC happens near the end of the AD process.

There's no time for them to assume the role of researcher, and that's work the AD writer has probably already done, anyway. So, instead of fixing everything themselves and duplicating effort, QC folks ask targeted questions that others can answer efficiently, like "Has this character been identified before?" and "What's the timecode of the first mention, so we can check name pronunciation here?" These questions are not accusations. They're a service to AD performers, writers, and sound engineers, so we can all do our best work.

I strongly believe that this crucial department is best filled by blind professionals. They know what will work for an AD audience because they *are* that audience. Experience in AD is important but, in a sense, secondary; people who care deeply about accessibility can gain exposure through training and volunteer work.[7]

People in both sound engineering and quality control tend to approach their roles with professionalism. It's inherent to their work, which is highly detailed and requires a great deal of focus. So naturally, as collaborators, they help the rest of us raise our AD game.

7 ADTrainingRetreats.com is an excellent skill-building resource for all things AD.

CHAPTER 5

Joining Forces with Production

Before we dive into this chapter about collaboration across the AD-production divide, let's step back and consider the worlds of film and TV. Compared with other visual media, they usually work with very different timetables, goals, and budgets. So, AD needs to flex with the format. It should be a direct reflection of the movie's or show's intent.

In other words, professionalism in AD involves bringing your best self to each project while also respecting its constraints.

If a student makes a video in their backyard with a smartphone and uploads it to YouTube, it might be a big hit with its target audience and even go viral. But the production quality is not going to match that of a superhero tentpole movie that costs hundreds of millions of dollars to make. That's OK. It's not trying to be that movie. You can still make the YouTube video accessible—and hats-off if you do!—but it doesn't call for anywhere near the same level of investment and professionalism.

TV and film projects are quite a big step up from that.

Let's face it, though: Throwing a bunch of money at a project does not guarantee accessibility. Many productions with healthy (or even obscene) budgets have sub-par AD. *That's* the challenge I'm forever trying to solve through my work and advocacy—and I've written this book partly in support of that goal. Although I wish your cousin all the best in his backyard film shoot with a total budget of one large cheese pizza and some cans of Pepsi, bringing more AD professionalism to that endeavor is not the focus here. We're trying to raise the bar in television and film.

To do that, we need to close some of the distance between the folks in AD and the producers calling the creative shots.

Several years ago, I performed AD on a few TV series that happened to be produced by friends of mine. When our paths crossed in regular life, I mentioned how great it was to work together—and they had no idea what I was talking about.

That's how separate our work worlds are.

Another time, when a producer friend asked me to perform AD on his feature film, it just so happened that I worked for the AD facility his studio used. I was so happy, thinking of how this connection—finally!—could support all parties: the AD facility, the production feature itself, and my own professional outreach. The AD facility recorded me on a section of an AD script.

Several weeks before the premiere, I got an email from my friend, asking, "Hey, I thought we were going to collaborate on AD on this film and promote our work on it together—what's up?" I didn't even flinch; at that time, AD facilities usually created just a week or so before the release date. But still, I was curious. While recording a different project at the AD facility, I told the engineer how excited I was to collaborate on the feature.

The engineer said, "Oh, we recorded that with someone else weeks ago."

I understand I might not have been the best fit, but how disappointing to have missed not only the outreach opportunity but also the communication. I felt an incredibly awkward feeling, going back to my friend and letting him know what had happened.

In each of these situations, I *knew* the people in production, and we *still* weren't communicating. We can only wonder how often that lack of interaction leads to missed opportunities for improvement in both the AD and the story.

Bill Sarine, filmmaker and cofounder of Beachglass Films, has this to say about the AD-production gap:

> I don't think a lot of filmmakers are thinking about AD as part of the film. It's [seen] like an accommodation for another audience....
>
> AD is basically a very subjective view of something that a filmmaker put a lot of deliberate effort into creating. So, there's a reason why the camera was on the floor when they walked into the room, or was on the ceiling, or was in their pocket, or whatever. There's a reason why we're in dark shadows, or we're in bright light, or we're in slow motion. There's a reason why all these choices are made on the filmmaking side, because it's part of that overall vision for how audiences are gonna take the story in. And so, AD—without the benefit of that input—is making decisions outside of that.
>
> I think AD pros are doing an amazing job, but I think that there is a disconnect there.[1]

---

1 https://www.roysamuelson.com/interviews/bill-sarine/

Yes, we've got some bridging to do. The first step, as they say, is awareness.

How The Industry (Mostly) Works

We've followed the process below for so long that most of us don't question it:

- A production company—the directors, the on-screen actors, the crew—creates the film itself.

- Then the film or show goes into postproduction (which is still, technically, part of production). This includes the sound editors, the sound mixers, the foley artists, the ADR mixer, the loop group performers who add background talk, the actors who re-record lines that didn't come through clearly—they each do their thing, and all that work is added to the production audio.

- Once postproduction is done—right before release to various streaming services, broadcasters, and/or theaters—the "final" creative product moves to the distributor. Traditionally, this is who hires one or more AD facilities to script, perform, record, and integrate the AD with the original audio.

You heard me right: It's the distributor—not the filmmaker, not the production team—who usually takes ownership of the AD work, after everything else is finished. So, there's little to no chance that the AD will inform the other creative work. And since all the outlets have their own relationships with the distributor (and with the multiple AD facilities that may or may not have their paws on the project), that just adds to the process complexity and makes it even harder to deliver AD that's true to the production's intent.

To illustrate some of the challenges that can crop up as a result, here's a quick example.

Remember I mentioned that sequel in a tentpole film series that shall still remain nameless has three versions of AD created by three different facilities? Yes, three—and that isn't unusual. As you might have guessed, the AD quality is uneven from one version to the next, and audiences have no way of knowing which one they'll get. Because of this lack of integration with the actual film, there isn't even a guarantee that AD will join the movie *at all* as it travels to various outlets.

It's as though we're on our own little AD island, with distribution ferries periodically coming and going, bringing us new projects to do and lugging our finished work away. A lot of that work might be good, but because it's done in relative isolation, it's bound to miss the mark in critical ways.

Making matters worse, AD facilities are disconnected from one another, as well. Largely for reasons of convenience and familiarity, each one has its own homegrown system. That not only increases the isolation but also ratchets up the complexity of the work and the amount of training (and retraining) needed to do it. The writers, performers, and sound and engineering pros who do audio description for a number of facilities—that is, most of us who do this work—must learn all the ins and outs of their various quirky processes. That takes time. It also results in confusion and mistakes.

Obstacles to Collaborating

If it were easy for production and AD to collaborate effectively, we'd already be doing it—right?

Well, I don't think difficulty is the main issue. I think it's hypercompartmentalization. The industry has put Baby in a corner, and to some extent we've cornered ourselves. From my perspective, after years of doing AD work, these are the related challenges we need to overcome.

Challenge 1: Perceived conflicts in goals and sensibilities

Because creative decision makers in production are busy doing their own jobs, they generally don't take much time to immerse themselves in the world of audio description. As a result, they may have preconceived notions about AD and assume there isn't much craft to it. While that's understandable—they've got a lot going on already, and we've all got areas we don't know much about —their limited awareness of what AD can do gets in the way of fruitful collaboration.

So, we need to look for opportunities to broaden their awareness a bit. Here's how Renee VanAusdall puts it:

> I would love for directors and for producers to understand that AD doesn't have to be this thing that they are reluctant about, because they don't wanna spoon-feed the story to people. You are not spoon-feeding anything if you do it well.
>
> If you bring that narrator in who feels like part of the story, and if you bring writers in who feel like they understand the tone of the story, and if you bring mixers in who can match what it is that your sound sounds like...if you can do that where they are part of the whole process, even from the beginning, then I think that the director is gonna actually be really pleased with this extra layer that they get to be part of in making sure

that people have the ability to hear that story.[2]

The crux of this challenge is getting decision makers to see AD folks as creative partners.

Challenge 2: The old "done and done" mentality when it comes to accessibility

The 21st Century CVAA (Communications and Video Accessibility Act) of 2010 required a certain number of hours of broadcast TV and theatrical releases to have audio description. That requirement became a box to check. As worthy and necessary as this mandate was, there was little incentive for the industry to go above and beyond. It was a huge and important step for blind audiences—but once the bar was set, it became "good enough."

Checking the box was an either/or choice: to have AD or not. Other factors, like how to do it well, whether to integrate it with production, and how much to invest in it, weren't considered. Those were—literally—outside the box.

Things are changing, I'm glad to say. Streaming services are choosing to include AD with no mandate to do so. More than 11,000 titles now have it as part of their distribution platform.

That's a great launching point, but we still have some distance to go. Including AD with all TV and film titles should be an inalienable feature. Until that happens, it will be tough for the industry to let go of the box-checking mentality and focus more on quality versus quantity in AD.

---

2 https://www.roysamuelson.com/interviews/renee-vanausdall

Challenge 3: There's always something else competing for resources

The creative value of the AD work—its potential to support the story being told—often gets sacrificed by resource cuts.

We've already talked about the "race to the bottom dollar" culture, but sometimes the challenge is more nuanced than that. When industry decision makers truly want to create accessible films and shows but find themselves up against a budget wall and have to make hard choices about what expenses to cut, they might decide to include AD but go "light" on the investment. They might see that as a tradeoff they can live with because it doesn't compromise overall quality, and the material is still "accessible."

The challenge is, *overall* quality does suffer for blind audiences, and so does accessibility. If the experience isn't as immersive as it is for sighted audiences, it's not really accessible.

Selling Executives on the Business Value of AD

Making sure blind audiences know they're in good hands with the audio description is a business decision. Until more entertainment executives see it that way, the industry will continue doing things as they're done now, farming out AD decisions to distributors, and their vendors, post-postproduction.

Remember, blind audience members are paying customers, and they voice their opinions on social media. Subpar AD results in subpar audience experiences, which can lead to negative reviews and comments online, fewer subscribers to streaming services, and fewer tickets sold at the Box Office—

all directly affecting the bottom line.[3] The opposite is true, too: Excellent AD makes for an immersive audience experience, and happy customers tend to be more profitable than unhappy ones.

If executives viewed AD as a potential money-maker, that would change the whole game. Audio description would be considered earlier, with appropriate levels of investment, and many roadblocks would be solved: Production budgets would allow for hiring real AD pros. The AD team (now looped into the production process) would have the information needed to do their best work. One high-quality version of the AD would travel with all the other elements of the film or show, from production to release to streaming. So, distribution would receive the AD content along with everything else, instead of hiring facilities to create it last-minute. And the AD track would be *built* to work well across the various streaming platforms.[4]

Yes, we're talking ideal world, but I've caught glorious glimpses of it in practice. For example, the latest SAG Awards included audio description for screening of nominated titles up for the awards, and the AD for the show was treated as an element of production. I participated in conversations about these changes with SAG Awards producers and with SAG-AFTRA's Performers with Disabilities Committee, and I appreciated how well these organizations worked together. It was exciting not only to help make all this happen for the awards show but also to start building closer relationships between AD and production folks.

---

3 AD audiences have family and friends, too. And, sighted people use AD for their own times away from screen: cooking, driving, cleaning, or just resting from screens, beyond other many uses of AD.

4 Each streaming service has its own requirements. Original production audio and video already have to accommodate them. AD would be no different.

Dreaming Big: What If AD Joined Production?

While including AD in the production process solves lots of challenges, it also creates a few. The tradeoffs are worth considering: The newly expanded production team has another set of responsibilities and tasks to manage, further complicating a process that's already quite layered. That team must also reengineer long-established workflows and build in new ways for departments to coordinate with the AD team.

Those changes tax the system, no doubt. But let's think about how it could benefit.

Richer audio overall

With accessibility more squarely in production's wheelhouse, more creative decisions bloom. Here's an example: the team incorporates more "audible images"—that is, audio effects behind the visuals—so there's less need for AD to explain and clarify what's happening on screen. To make a remote beach scene more accessible, for instance, production brings in sounds of seagulls and waves and children laughing in the distance. Why tell when you can show with sound? Audible images give audiences (whether blind or sighted) another way to process the story. When people aren't inundated with description of visual details, they can breathe a little easier— and sit with the emotions they're meant to feel.

Better AD

When the production team owns AD, the director and producer are right there to clarify intent and focus our efforts. They have us adjust performances that are too big or too narrow for the scene. They call breaks when we need them but don't realize it. And they pay us a minimum wage, like they pay other SAG-

AFTRA performers.

In other words, they support us so we can deliver our best work. With fewer basic mistakes to find and fix later, quality control can focus on fine tuning. What a luxury.

Mutual trust

A good director trusts—and is trusted by—the entire production team to represent the story being told. Having and earning faith in one another is the proverbial rising tide that lifts all kinds of boats, like productivity, resourcefulness, engagement, and quality. With AD in production, buoyed by that same tide, we reap those benefits, too, as creative partners.

Joe Strechay, a film producer and vocal advocate for bringing accessibility and inclusion into production, trusts and values his AD colleagues. As a coproducer on *See*, an Apple TV+ series, here's how he removed barriers to collaboration:

> In my work as co-producer for season two, I started…talking to the consumers around the United States and abroad about the audio description and what that experience was. And as a person who was there helping to block the scenes for season one, and then hearing the AD, I felt the [AD team] didn't have contact with the production. So, they [only] go off of what they see in the actual cut. And they don't always know exactly what we're trying to do or what specific world we've created.
>
> So, during season two, I brought it up to Apple. I said, I would really love to have a conversation with the folks that decide on the AD for our production and see if there's anything we can do to work together to make it even better.

And they came back, and they said yes. Sarah Herrlinger at Apple and some of the executives championed it and really let me have that conversation. But also, once we started having that conversation, we decided that I was gonna get involved in audio description. I was gonna go through the cuts and look for that world-specific information.

First we provided them information that we thought could have been more detailed for our world in the show. And then I started going through the cuts with my assistant; she would describe what was on the screen, and then I'd know what we were trying to do in that, and what would come across, like someone holding their hand up at a specific point.

It might just look like they're holding it up, like maybe they're feeling the temperature of the fire as they're passing it, or maybe they are using lower body protective technique. So, we started describing it, just making, and giving, those world-specific pieces.[5]

By working so closely with AD, Strechay provided a lot of contextual detail that was missing the prior season. Perhaps more important than that, he established mutual trust and respect with the audio description team.

Their collaborative process has evolved from there:

I don't write the AD scripts. I don't write audio description. I just write some bullet points about each scene, things that I would like covered in

---

5 https://www.roysamuelson.com/interviews/joe-stretchay/

that scene or that will help paint that picture from my viewpoint.

Sometimes it's about costumes. Sometimes it's about things that might not always make it.... I wanted our audio description to be more detailed than typical audio description.

You'll see it as the season goes on. We get more and more detailed. You're gonna see more little Easter eggs put in there too...something you don't just get from the screen. So, we're breaking some audio description rules, but I'm taking that liberty and I really pushed for it.[6]

Breaking rules together? Sounds like progress to me.

A culture of learning

With AD in production, we also learn more from one another day to day. How nice is *that*?

It takes humility and a willingness to make and fix mistakes openly. While these attitudes aren't necessarily easy to adopt, they're rewarding. And they reinforce the idea that we're all on the same team, not "us" over here trying to work with "them" over there.

On one film I produced AD for, we had a team of five people plus a producer and a director who were hands-on. The writer created a brilliant AD script, the QC pass cleared up a few errors, and the performer was directed clearly and explicitly. After another two QC passes by the specialist and me, we handed the AD track off to the director and the producer for review on the sound editing side. It wasn't until then that the sound editor caught a name that changed pronunciation after

6 https://www.roysamuelson.com/interviews/joe-strechay

a handful of cues.

Thankfully, our team responded. We quickly fixed the mistake and redelivered the file. We were surprised that we had all missed it—but once it was noted, it was clear as day.

What had happened? The writer had updated her operating system, and the app she used defaulted to autocorrect without her knowledge. The uniquely spelled name transformed into a similar-sounding name—in thousands of sentences that the AD performer read as written.

Five pros who know the business missed this error. But mistakes happen, and people are human. The producer and the director understood. We all gave each other some grace, with no blame or shame. We treated this as a moment of discovery: we'd learned how the system could introduce errors. Going forward, we'd be better equipped to catch similar mistakes.

In a future idealized world, AD is owned by, and included in, production and post-production. AD writers are part of the Writer's Guild of America, benefiting from protections and consistencies of compensation for the high value they give. AD performers are covered under similar contracts, and paid at least a minimum wage. The production trusts the AD facilities to guide them where the AD audiences want. Release dates include this AD, and the AD talents that worked on production are both named and celebrated for their contributions. The AD travels along.

The entertainment business isn't perfect, and AD is a part of that business. But with focus, effort, care, and professionalism, all departments can work together to deliver a superb movie or show that immerses the audience in the story.

And working together is a skill in itself.

CONCLUSION
Let's Connect, Shall We?

Audio description's core driver is helping people connect—both with the story being told and with others who are sharing that experience in living rooms, theaters, and the world beyond. We know that. It's what motivates many of us to do this essential work.

But to do it as well as it deserves to be done, we also need to connect—with fellow AD pros and with colleagues in other departments and functions. Everyone working together, learning from one another, trading notes and observations, sharing experiences, appreciating one another's contributions, offering support in all the little ways we can—that's how we'll fuel healthy growth and change in the industry.

Carl Richardson, co-chair of the Audio Description Project, describes some of his organization's efforts in that vein:

> Basically, we are an advocacy arm of ACB, the American Council of the Blind, where we pro-

mote awareness of Audio Description and work with companies, vendors, and consumers to increase the amount of audio description available to consumers.

That can [include] negotiating with streaming services to get audio description, [for instance, or] letting consumers know what titles are available on television and film....

We also do stuff for theaters, museums, and visitor centers, and educate young blind students about the benefits of audio description. We have an essay contest every year with middle school and high school students where we ask them to watch [a show or movie with] audio description and write an essay about it.[1]

Coming at this issue from different angles—advising content creators on accessibility, lobbying for resources, educating audiences about tools that are available—is such a smart approach. Richardson has his sights set on technical innovation, too. "One thing that is exciting," he says, "is we are starting to see apps with audio description tracks on your phone, so that if you go to a movie or watch television, you can use your own personal device." He has also pushed for change at the federal level: the Audio Description Project "was very much involved in the creation of the 21st Century Communications and Video Accessibility Act, otherwise known as the CVAA, which mandates that the four broadcast networks and the five top-rated cable networks produce 87 and a half hours a quarter."

He's connecting lots of dots—and people—to get things done. He's increasing equitable access to entertainment, one

---

1 https://www.roysamuelson.com/interviews/carl-richardson/

conversation at a time.

Some AD pros are looking for progress within their areas of expertise. For example, sound engineer Jeff Ross has been thinking about ways to get content providers in sync on production values. If big industry players set clear, high standards for their AD tracks, he points out, it becomes easier for others to follow suit:

> Within one company, they may own 50 production companies' worth of content. So, it seems to me this is a good time across the board to set a standard—at, say, Netflix or Amazon, that's the type of company I'm talking about—and that brings all this content together into one place. Of course, they want to be standardized; from program to program, they want to sound similar. It would be very strange if they sounded very different.[2]

It takes coordination to make meaningful strides toward accessibility. So, I've been organizing and participating in initiatives like Kevin's Way[3] and TheADNA.org[4] to help industry colleagues see how high-quality AD can affect their creative work for the better. I've seen successes, but as with any endeavor that starts off like a bunch of wet noodles thrown at a wall, some things don't stick. When they don't, it can be demoralizing. But when they do, it's energizing.

When I need to find motivation to keep advocating, Renee VanAusdall, our resident AD enthusiast, is right there to as-

---

2 https://www.roysamuelson.com/interviews/jeff-ross/

3 This began as a push for more standardization and professionalism in audio description and has since pivoted to focus on crediting all roles in AD for film and TV. For more detail, go to https://kevinsway.com/ and see appendix, "The Story of Kevin's Way: Some Excerpts."

4 I founded this organization to get industry pros working together toward shared accessibility goals.

sure me that it matters:

> I'm learning about all these different communities, and people who are involved. I am so grateful for all of the people who put time into audio description, any part of their week, any part of their day invested in making things more accessible and inclusive. That just makes me so happy to know that we are not being forgotten as members of the blind community. We are not being quieted. We have a voice.[5]

And Fern Lulham, a blind performer, is there to remind me how far we've actually come:

> I've always been a big believer that you shouldn't point the finger, you shouldn't say everything's bad and everything's terrible. Absolutely stand up if something is inaccessible, but also celebrate when something is really accessible, when it is working, when it is going well.[6]

That's the good fight we're fighting together. But how can we collaborate even more effectively? By addressing underrepresentation and becoming better allies.

Addressing Underrepresentation

It's a given—culturally and systemically—that people without disabilities don't have to fight nearly as hard as those with disabilities to have their voices heard and their needs met.

---

5 https://www.roysamuelson.com/interviews/renee-vanausdall/
6 https://www.roysamuelson.com/interviews/fern-lullham/

As a general rule, the sighted are very well represented in this world. Blind audiences, not so much, and that costs them time and energy and frustration. The same goes for blind voice performers who seek training, jobs, and professional growth. They're nowhere near parity.

Often without realizing it, sighted industry professionals create obstacles for disabled performers. They may blissfully assume the playing field is level when it's anything but. They may, with good intentions and bad judgment, throw blind colleagues into high-stakes situations unequipped to succeed. Because of the cultural bias, sometimes sighted performers can recover more readily when they fail. For one thing, they're given, on average, a lot more chances to prove themselves, so one bad work experience isn't as likely to derail their career. For another, they have easier access to safe "playgrounds" like workshops and readings where they can build skills and confidence.

Of course, the fewer blind professionals we have doing audio description, the less informed our work is. To make entertainment more accessible, we need their perspective, which means we need to advocate for equitable professional opportunities in the AD world.

Becoming Better Allies

The most important thing we can do as allies is to bring blind professionals into our skill-building environments (those safe playgrounds we were just talking about) and include them in all aspects of AD creation. Writing, performing, engineering, editing, quality control—each department can benefit a great deal from their experience as consumers of AD content.

That isn't to say we should be all Kumbaya about it. There

are real challenges to address—I've described many of them in this book. Nor, as Fern Lulham pointed out, should we wag our fingers at companies and colleagues whose practices are less than inclusive. That's not the way to get them on board. Instead, we need real conversations between blind and sighted colleagues, where we wrestle with difficult questions and search for honest answers.

Inclusion and conversation—those are two big ways to make a difference. What are some smaller things we can do day-to-day?

We can think about how we show up in the world and go about our usual activities. For example, many of us are active social media users. What are your social media habits? Do you consistently capitalize the first letter of each word within hashtags to make them easier for people on the blindness spectrum to read? Do you describe images with alt text? These may seem like the tiniest of steps, but they really can help disabled performers and other professionals access any learning or job opportunities you're sharing online.

As for doing the work itself, keep training and keep bringing your best. Study with people who know what they are talking about. Continue to sharpen your skills in workshops and classes. Network on the regular to build relationships, gain perspective, and avoid siloed thinking and working. And if you're in a position to include AD folks in the credits, do it.

Giving Credit Where It's Due

Explicitly acknowledging AD pros along with all the other contributors to a show or film sends an important signal to the audience and to the industry: it says their work is valuable and valued.

In the entertainment business, we all need credits. Our livelihood depends on them. Historically, voice actors have struggled to get recognition for roles. Just ask Adriana Caselotti, the actress who gave us the voice of Snow White in the original animated Disney film. Never heard of her? That's because the studio didn't allow her to let anyone know about her role in the movie. According to ScreenRant: "This was done with the intention of preserving the magic, with Walt Disney allegedly wanting to only have the voice of a character associated with the animated version, rather than with a real person."[7] It's no surprise that Caselotti's career suffered as a result.

How silly that rule seems by today's standards. It's equally silly that AD pros often don't get the credits they deserve.

But progress is coming on that front. Recently, Netflix added language to its audio description style guide about crediting AD work: "Include AD post-house name, scriptwriter, and voice talent credits within the AD track, after the last frame of picture of the main program and before the end credit crawl."[8]

AD credits will become the norm, not the exception. As this work gains recognition, I'm hoping that we'll make other gains as well—in resources allocated, in skills developed, in careers built, and, most of all, in audiences reached.

Because it's all connected.

7 https://screenrant.com/disney-princess-department-ruined-adriana-caselotti-career/

8 https://partnerhelp.netflixstudios.com/hc/en-us/articles/215510667-Audio-Description-Style-Guide-v2-5

Roy Samuelson

AUTHOR BIO

With his ability to fuse emotional resonance with inclusive storytelling, Roy ensures blind people enjoy watching videos.

By consulting with companies and creators to elevate storytelling for all audiences he crafts immersive experiences beyond meeting standards, allowing for greater engagement, and emotional impact.

Since 2014, Roy has performed on thousands of AD projects for film and TV and has worked with dozens of AD facilities on those projects. He uses his decades of experience in entertainment media to pursue parity for AD professionals and audiences alike. His podcast—"The ADNA Presents," with more than 200 episodes—features AD professionals in all departments, and showcases underrepresented talents in film and TV.

A 2021 Audio Description Achievement Award recipient, Roy has presented multiple times at American Council of the Blind, National Federation of the Blind, and American Foundation for the Blind. Most recently, he developed AD from the ground up in collaboration with filmmakers for the upcoming American Federation for the Blind production "Possibilities," directed and produced by Beachglass Films.

Roy consults with organizations on integrating AD within their video content. He also provides one-on-one coaching for voice performers who are interested in AD work, along with accessible workouts that feature feedback from blind professionals.

In his ongoing efforts to set and maintain the highest standards for AD, Roy:

- Demonstrates expertise in AD performance and training using this very book

- Founded the Audio Description Discussion Group – Leading a community of 3,500+ with lively conversations focused on AD quality and excellence

- Hosts "The ADNA Presents" Podcast – Showcasing over 200 episodes of underrepresented AD talents in film and TV

- Delivered the keynote speech for the American Council of the Blind—Advocating for quality over quantity in AD, broke out the departments in AD, and highlighted the inclusion of blind professionals

- Served on the TV Academy Performers Peer Group Executive Committee – Leading the initiative to include AD performers' credits for Emmy eligibility

- Produced the Television Academy Panel on AD – Reinforcing thought leadership by organizing industry discussions

- Received the 2021 Audio Description Achievement Award – Recognizing his significant contributions to the AD industry

- Facilitated SAG Awards Screeners with AD – Advocating for AD in nominated films, supporting blind talents and audiences

- Performed voice-over in thousands of blockbuster films and TV series – Possessing deep understanding of best practices across AD facilities

Roy has a nuanced expertise in balancing voices to create inclusive, emotionally impactful storytelling through audio description (AD).This expertise positions him not only as a consultant who helps companies navigate the complexities of voice integration but also as someone who champions accessibility as a strategic advantage.

He's not just offering technical solutions—he's helping companies unlock new markets, deepen audience engagement, and enhance brand loyalty through the irreplaceable emotional power of human voices, while guiding them through the appropriate use of AI.

))),

ACKNOWLEDGEMENTS

I'm thankful for the many alliances, from 1in4 Coalition, to Bold Blind Beauty, and many dear and talented colleagues and friends, like Eli Schiff, Kelly Brennan, Mike DeBonis, Steve Letnes, Douglas Sarine, Cathy Lind Hayes, and the many AD facilities who collaborate, share, and focus their efforts; thanks for trusting me with your words, and sharing your own words.

Nicholas DeWolff for strategic vision – his support, guidance, and clarity have erased a lot of fumblings, weeds, and diversions. Beyond focus, his care and support exceed any high expectations I had in our initial collaboration.

Serina Gilbert for behind the scenes conversations, thoughtful pragmatism, deep understanding, and music recommendations.

Jamie Saxton for the seemingly effortless support, research, virtual emotional shoulder, perspective enhancer, and "oh, we got this" attitude. I consistently look at the help she's provided for these and many more efforts.

Claudette Sutherland for her patience in her writing work-shops, and wealth of experience in the entertainment indus-try, and life. The no-nonsense, the light, and the joy always shine.

Bill Sarine for listening to the many challenges, and picking up the mantle.

Paul Zakarian for his extra caring, practical help, and endless "how can I help you"s.

Colleen Connor, because they get it, and know how to sharp-en the rainbow when it needs to, and dull my extra sharp-ness when I needed chill pills.

Bridget Melton for all things AD: getting it, growing it, and amplifying it.

Zach Thomas for caring collaboration, and delivering great work under impossible circumstances.

Kevin Thompson for everything, and remaining with me beyond his earthly departure. This is all for you, dear friend.

Russ Marleau for showing me trust, love, care, and beautiful discussions. Thanks for the laughs, the perspective changes, and being there more times than I can count. You gave to so many others; I miss you my friend.

Vivian Syroyezhkin for the multiple passes, the several starts from scratch, the structure, the feedback, the direction, and billion light blub moments she pointed toward.

Rebecca Odum for the sensitivity pass that confirmed more than I expected.

Joie Samuelson Miller (for her effortless (and meticulous) work — which, hopefully — gives a final grade, that passes. These sentences: Are clearly exempt. As they should be.)

Vicki Hoskins, for stepping out of retirement for a minute with further thoughts.

For all the interviewees on The ADNA Presents, for sharing their experience, and propelling AD in film and TV further along.

Tres Williams for doing thousands of jobs and still making time to get what needs to be done done.

Stephanae McCoy for every inappropriate laugh, deep connection, and extra thoughts I'd not considered before.

Bob Bergen, for getting the AD qualifications done, but beyond that, for being a solid sounding board, and bringing practical, next step advice. You've never steered me wrong.

Satauna Howery, for knowing we should have recorded every conversation of ours for the benefit of those who would have the privilege of knowing your approaches. Thanks for being right.

Melissa Exelberth for historical perspectives on the voice over industry, her cutthroat pass on this very book (I'm so glad you at least liked the writing when others were quoted), and for guiding this to where it could be; thanks for being real with me as always, it changes me for the better.

Scriptwrights, from Sam Rawlings and her continued legacy, and Scott Mullen, Debra Rogers, Warren Leonard, John Rixey Moore, and the many produced writers who continue to knock it out. Thanks for the many great opportunities to bring your characters and stories to life.

Hedy Burress for the many laughs, and heartfelt conversations.

April Watts for her many unexpected gifts of perspectives, ideas, kindness, listening ear, the warm heart, and compassion. Plus she is a power performer. She is also sunshine.

Sara Stuckey for getting this started.

Inger Tudor for laughs and talking me off ledges.

Dave Wallace for understanding this work, and rolling with it to where it can go. Your skills from the workshop to where you are now are so not surprising.

The Television Academy for getting done one of my career dreams: including AD performers TV credits to qualify to join the illustrious organization, and for the panels articles and more. Inclusion is working.

SAG Awards producers, from Jon and Jen to the many others - your openness, willingness to pioneer requirements that have spillover effects for the industry at large, and your growth mindset that continues to make accessibility even better with each passing year.

Dr. Joel Snyder - for getting the ball rolling some 3 decades ago, creating opportunities for the dozens of AD professionals, and for each shift of inclusion you've listened to and embraced.

GB for introducing me to the kind, loving, and aware community, and everyone there.

Heather Warren, Joshua Loya, Chad Allen, Heather Foster, Lynne Thomas, Isaac Jean-Paul for the book title ideas and keeping me going through some patches.

Juan Alcazar for his creativity, thoughtfulness, care, compassion, and drive.

Brandon Cole. Your legacy will always pave ways.

Melody Goodspeed, for your friendship, support, and AD snobbery.

Brett Paesel for being so chill, smart, vulnerably clever, and just what this book needed at just the perfect time.

Lisa Burrell for surgical precision, the gift of her expertise, and such trusted collaboration. When this book soars, skips along, and ties together, it's thanks to her expertise and decisive cuts, unearthing what I was trying to say.

Christin Lee, for putting it together, laying it out.

Julia Bianco Schoeffling, for the talks, the neighborliness, the publishing, and guidance in so many ways.

Alex Smith for the grounding smiles and Sunshine.

)))

APPENDICES

)))

References You Might Find Useful

ON AUDIO DESCRIPTION AS A TRADE AND A CRAFT:

The ADNA Presents podcast (more than 200 interviews of AD professionals)

http://theadna.org/the-adna-presents

The ADNA Presents "Know Your Narrator" collection

https://www.amazon.com/dp/B09MZB7K2T/ref=cm_sw_em_r_
mt_dp_N90AQBEV0VJP7J3KJTFK

Database of audio description professionals in film and TV

https://www.theADNA.org

What is Audio Description?

https://www.adtrainingretreats.com/what-is-audio-description

ON AI AND AD:

Beyond Words: Emotion AI's Revolutionary Impact on Professional Communication

https://www.forbes.com/sites/rhettpower/2023/12/26/beyond-words-emotion-ais-revolutionary-impact-on-professional-communication

2024 Labor Innovation & Technology Summit: AI Goes To Hollywood

https://www.youtube.com/watch?v=XuV-guyqHcU&t=4418s

The Uncanny Valley: Advancements and Anxieties of AI That Mimics Life

https://www.forbes.com/sites/bernardmarr/2024/02/07/the-uncanny-valley-advancements-and-anxieties-of-ai-that-mimics-life/?sh=3b1bd15e5f96

AD TTS speech

https://www.instagram.com/p/CNIvDrnJ3Co/

And a sample comparison

https://www.roysamuelson.com/human-ad-and-synth-voice-ad-comparison/

ON THE MINDSET WE BRING TO OUR WORK:

Tim LeBon on How Altruistic Perfectionism Is Self-Defeating

https://podcasts.apple.com/us/podcast/80-000-hours-podcast/id1245002988?i=1000608523408

ON ROY:

Articles and Interviews

https://www.roysamuelson.com/articles-and-interviews/

An audio description primer — super great storytelling, and features myself and some colleages

https://www.20k.org/episodes/athousandwords

The ADNA Presents Know Your Narrator Series:
Roy Samuelson

https://www.youtube.com/watch?v=YBjTPSWjTXs

In the world of AD rant

https://www.instagram.com/p/CrHlHNNpKfi/

My licensing plan for audio description identification

https://www.kevinsWay.com (my licensing plan for audio description identification)

AD Portfolio

https://www.roysamuelson.com/coaching/#ADPortfolio

Partial AD performance credit list

https://theADNA.org/roy-samuelson

Advocacy and outreach on AD

https://roysamuelson.com/news

Comic-Con panel — I explain AD and the complexities our audiences are faced with

https://roysamuelson.com/comic-con-panel-2024

Text to Speech
("To Perform is Human; to Synth, Malign")

Ok, but what about AI?

If we can't tell the difference between disengaged AI and amateur human performance, either way there's something really wrong with the performance. And at this point, that's where we are with the technology.

Currently, synth voices bring a wealth of opportunity for purely informational AD. But in entertainment media, where stories and characters are built in, AD's job extends beyond simply saying words to channeling and matching emotions. While AI may eventually learn to read complex contextual clues and adjust its performance appropriately, it's still learning how to pronounce names correctly. Many QC specialists find the workarounds to that problem tedious and challenging. AI keeps calling my friend Stephanae McCoy (founder of Bold Blind Beauty) "Stephage"—kind of like Stonehenge, but not. Sure, text-to-speech errors can be fixed by a human... but doesn't that add another layer of confusion, cost, and delay?

Human AD performers make mistakes. But they don't

glitch, they invest in their own programming and maintenance, and they're worlds ahead on delivering immersive audience experiences.

Here's what Mac The Movie Guy had to say about the difference in quality in a review of a prominent film that featured synth voice AD:

> The script is nearly inaudible at times and at other times chooses to dominate the movie's soundtrack to make the movie inaudible. Its balancing is baffling, because it usually is one or the other, but there were sequences where the sound dropped out for the audio description... and there were times where the AD was nearly inaudible... Sometimes, the AI actually sounds like it's mumbling, like it had one too many drinks before hopping on to narrate. But it is a very obvious fake voice that was never mixed properly and certainly wasn't quality checked.

> You don't get an award for making broken accessibility. No one pats a business on the back for putting...grip rails in nonuseful places, or worse, not making sure they aren't anchored to the wall to be able to sustain weight. No one gets recognition for building wheelchair ramps that take you to just one little stair you still have to roll over...

> Remember, sighted people often choose movies or television programs as entertainment and an escape from their day. It is not an escape from our day when we spend all day working with awful robotic screen readers and then kick back...and have to listen to the audio description

equivalent of Smallpox.[1]

John Stark posted that in January 2024. Clearly, audience experience can suffer when you take away the human AD performer.

Again, in contexts where people are simply looking for information, not entertainment, AI is fine. There are some really compelling arguments to be made for text to speech for straight-up facts.

I want to know what my calendar is. Or I want to know what my email says. Who wants a human performer for that?

But when I'm engaging with stories on television or film, when there's an element of emotion, when I want to fully be immersed in the experience—things are different. A human voice does the job better.

Still, for argument's sake, let's say you try using text to speech in your next AD project, because you're looking to cut costs and save time.

Now, obviously you need to build—or buy and adapt—the software. A lot of companies have done that. And that's great.

You also have to maintain the software. Upgrade it and make sure that all the bugs are out. Voice talents get upgrades, too, with their training and coaching, so that's kind of a wash.

But enhancing audience experience—that whole "true accessibility" thing we've been talking about—gets tricky with text to speech. Take this sample audio description line:

John gives April the red apple.

In that sentence, a lot of things might be happening.

John might be giving the red apple to April instead of Susan. In that case, we would want to subtly emphasize the recipient's name: John gives APRIL the red apple.

Or what if it's usually someone else who gives the apple to April? Then we want to convey that John is the giver this time:

1 https://macthemovieguy.com/2024/01/06/foe-the-review-to-end-all-reviews/

JOHN gives April the red apple.

What if it's happening in a room full of green apples? In that context, it's important to emphasize the color: John gives April the RED apple.

Or maybe John typically gives April a different kind of fruit, like an orange, but this time it's an apple. Then: John gives April the red APPLE.

Or maybe he usually steals it from her: John GIVES April the red apple.

To accent the right word in text-to-speech AD, all you have to do is highlight it in the sentence, so the software knows what to do with it. No problem.

But you also have to figure out where to place the line. For example, if there's a comedic beat where John is giving April the red apple, it's gotta be timed so that the AD audience is in on the joke.

Again, that's simple to program. You just have to put it in. Someone's got to do it, but that's cool. You can handle that.

Then there's the mood of the scene. If it's at the end of a sad romantic movie and—God forbid—April's about to die, that line about the apple can't be delivered in a standard conversational tone. It's going to be jarring to the audience emotionally. It's going to take them out of the scene.

If it's a super-funny moment in the movie—and the voice is just conversational—that won't fly, either. It'll take the audience out of the story in a different way.

Tone is programmable, too. You might have like 16 different choices. I personally choose from a list of around 200 intentions that I bring as a voice talent when I do audio description. But OK, you go with one of the 16. Or you ramp up your investment in programming (and subsequent upgrading and troubleshooting and quality-checking) to expand the list to 200.

Once you've done all that, you can move on to the next five

sentences of that cue—and then tackle all the other cues. In a typical movie or TV show, there could be hundreds of cues. So that's thousands of sentences where you tell the computer which words to emphasize, where to place the line, how to time the delivery, and what tone to use.

Can you remind me what we're saving by replacing human beings (who could be blind talents) with text to speech in AD?

I've heard some authentic-sounding synth voices—don't get me wrong. The technology has come a long way. If I can watch three seasons of a TV show and only during season 4 realize that the describer was not a human performer, then I'd say that the production is, at least for me, a success. But we're not there yet. And when we do get there, it won't be cheap.

)))

The Weakest Link

A few years ago, frustrated after hearing sub-par AD on countless feature films and TV series, I took a deep, cleansing breath and posted the following aspirational invitation on social media:

Shout out to you AD professionals.

Excellent quality AD can't have any weak links.

Any of these could be dealbreakers:

Audio Description script word choice.

Placement of those words.

Rate of words (how many words, how fast).

Emphasis of words. (Is it "she ate the red * APPLE * or she ate the * RED * apple? Is it the fruit or the color of the apple?)

Intention of words. (This is where the voice talent brings her skills to the table. Some call this emotion, but it's intention—a performance craft that is active.)

Clarity of words.

Support of the story.

Casting of the voice.

The voice's professional and ongoing training.

The placement of the audio cues.

The mix of the audio (how loud or soft it is in your ear).

How it aligns with production.

The quality control—consistency of words.

How the AD fits in the mind of the audience.

The necessary elements of the story.

Not stepping on or interrupting the emotional silences.

Then it's gotta travel from "cinema to streaming to streaming."

Then it's gotta be accessible.

So, there are 18 elements right there, and the countless hours of training and experience and ability to deliver this on deadline.

There are more elements than these 18! But in this example, if 17 are spectacular, and if even one of them isn't great, it can negatively affect your entire AD experience.

Thank you to all the professionals who put in the time and care to do their part to not be the weakest link.

)))

Audio Description Panel Follow-up for SOVAS 2022

The Society of Voice Arts and Sciences (SOVAS) invited several AD professionals to speak about their craft and the challenges they face. Here, edited for clarity and length, are my responses to some of the panel's questions:

Can you comment on the unique nature of performing for audio description compared with other voiceover genres?

For film and TV, AD performance requires a combination of a lot of VO skills. Taking words off a page, cold reading, timing, and professionalism are all key to being a success… But most important is a nuanced and subtle performance that doesn't get in the way. I coach VO performers to find that sweet spot, and it's a high-wire act! The performance doesn't sound like a performance; it doesn't stand out, yet fully supports the story being told.

Presentational reads and cold, sleepy reads are both "tells" that an AD performer is inexperienced. And voice pros who sound like they like the sound of their own voice? Always a bad fit for this work.

While the AD voice talent is most often working with a director/producer in a recording session, do you think that there is a kind of synergy between the writer and the voice talent? How does one depend on the other to create effective audio description?

Anymore, I'm usually reading to picture on my own. When I am directed, particularly for well-known series that can't release the video to the AD crew, the engineer and director in the studio guide the performance and make sure that the words are correctly read.

Regardless, it's a team effort with the writer who has given us the AD script, usually at the last minute. That writing makes all the difference. A great AD writer not only will find the essential visual elements to include but also will choose the right words and sentence lengths, among many other decisions. A skilled writer makes the AD script language fit the content.

In the script, I'm given:

- Actual words to say, obviously.

- Timecodes that indicate when to record. If the total cue length isn't included, I do a lot of math to figure out how long these cues are! Sometimes I use software that automates the process, similar to ADR recording, or dubbing.

- Pauses within cues, either to allow some needed silence or to make room for audio (dialogue, explosions, other elements).

- Dynamics for cues, like "brisk" or "fast" (and directions for the rare but inevitable times when the AD has to talk over dialogue).

- Pronunciations.

- And much more.

In addition to the above, a good AD writer fits the words in without rushing all the lines. I average around 1,000 cues for 4 hours of content. I've done 100 cues, around 1,300 words, in 13 minutes. So, all this moves very fast.

How can the folks who are here—beginners as well as veteran voice actors—pursue work as voice talents for audio description projects?

I'd begin by strongly recommending that you, as a VO professional, consider your motivations. It's important not to see this as charity work. "Helping blind people" might feel good, but it can come across as a better-than-thou attitude, which no one wants. And that attitude does come out in reads—they sound condescending or presentational.

Our role as voice professionals is to give access to the visuals in a way that doesn't get in the way of the story. And reading as if you, the voice, are the show? That will definitely get in the way.

Practicing cold reading is essential. You need to tune your instrument and hear yourself back as you do this work.

Finally, connect with audiences and people who work in the industry. The culture of AD has changed dramatically, evolving with the wants and needs of our audiences. Pay attention to what they want and find ways to deliver that.

As you pursue opportunities in AD, be a learner. I'm still being coached myself. With those acting chops honed, and voiceover specifics cultivated, you'll find jobs. There are more than 8,700 projects in TV and film with AD, and countless opportunities for live events, museums, educational materials, and corporate content. So, know that scarcity isn't a factor; don't fight for crumbs. Stand for what you know is right and acknowledge your own good work. Celebrate the small wins. Brené Brown's research shows that if we don't acknowledge incremental successes, we increase our risk of burnout. So, celebrate those little steps. This applies to all aspects of VO!

Also, vet your assumptions with others who have worked for the companies you're pursuing as clients. I can't tell you how many voice professionals have shared poor experiences with some sketchy AD facilities. There are, sadly, consistencies in their stories.

For example, getting paid fairly for this work can be challenging, especially if you aren't working with a solid facility. To avoid unexpected roadblocks, clarify the following up front:

- Will you do short turnaround times?

- Will you get paid for rerecording an entire script because of major rewrites or something as simple as a name change for a lead character?

- Will you accommodate last-minute scripts that aren't formatted?

- Will you do the engineer's job and place each cue to picture?

- Will you be available at the drop of a hat, even when it conflicts with personal commitments or other professional obligations?

These and many more variables directly affect your time investment and your ability to complete tasks. They should affect your payment, too.

Get everything in writing. (Yes, email counts.) That way, if there's ever a question about what's agreed upon, you have an easy way to clear up the confusion.

I'm in regular contact with a dozen reputable AD facilities that work in film and TV. Through my conversations and work experiences, I've learned that each company has its own approach to writing, performing, recording, and editing AD. You have to be ready to adapt and know what you're getting into. I've seen many skilled VO performers who will likely never work for certain AD facilities because of their generalized approach.

Most AD companies are actively seeking writers. Their pool of voice pros is fairly deep, but you can still break through. That's partly what I focus on in my workouts and coaching sessions—skills that will set you apart.

Sign up at roysamuelson.com for coaching opportunities with inclusive voiceover workouts for blind and sighted pros.

The Story of Kevin's Way: Some Excerpts

Every time I've mentioned my fear of using Kevin's name in a way that might be construed as manipulative or disingenuous or, worse, inspiration porn, I'm reminded why his name carries such weight in the business. Our brand "Kevin's Way" honors his legacy. And it honors our relationship, too. He was my anchor, my mentor, and my friend who I loved.

He'd smile and shake his head at hearing that, I'm sure, then turn on some Casey Kasem top 40, knowing we'd share more text messages, phone calls, and conversations about all this.

———

[His mom] told me about the morning that Kevin's elementary school bus never showed, and she had to take him on the Atlanta commuter train.

She said she held his hand as they boarded. She sat next to him on an adjacent seat. If he had ever had eyes, he'd've rolled them.

At the closest stop to the school, he stood up.

"Kevin, you want me to take you to school?"

He took out his cane and smiled, shaking his head. "Mother, you can stay on."

He walked off the train, but his mom couldn't resist. He started down the sidewalk. And she followed quietly, concerned for his safety.

She said Kevin walked, and she walked.

Kevin stopped at every red light and made his way to the school. (I still hear her laughing, as she recalled that time when he was 5 years old... He ran down the stairs to his ham and cheese sandwich, she taking her time. "That's how he'd do. He can get around.")

At the school, she saw the teacher open the door for him. "Kevin, I see your mother!"

"Yeah, I know. I smelled her cologne."

She continued:

"He got around so good, and it made me feel good he was doing stuff. I couldn't baby him. I let him play with kids. He fell down and got back up. Everyone said his mama let him do that. Ain't nothing gonna hold him back."

As an adult, he traveled from Atlanta to Jackson.

He would go and come, and visit his friend.

And she said he tried to keep stuff from her. He didn't want her to know anything about it.

A year before he died, she knew something was wrong. He was having problems. Something was going on. The only thing holding him back – his ankles started swelling. He gotta check that out.

———

About two years ago, Kevin contacted me via a Facebook

private message, writing, "I am constantly spreading the word about how blind people watch movies, and I love your narration of that. If there's ever anything that I can do to help with the cause, please don't hesitate to reach out. Thank you again for everything that you do."

My narration for audio description wasn't known by many, and I was reaching out wherever I could, talking about it. Here was someone responding. It wasn't a bot. Wow, he's real. It felt great to connect with someone.

I offered to pass along any suggestions or feedback to my coworkers. He wrote that he had heard my voice hundreds of times over the last few seasons. He was curious about the whole process.

As the exchanges continued, and grew longer in each of our responses, we talked about dating, and he mentioned being on a date that stood him up. With truth and humor, he said, "I don't know if he walked out because I was blind, too tall, black, or gay—and he needed to run back into the closet."

A lot of times when he met sighted people, it didn't go well.

He told me, "Today, a waitress went up to my table and meekly said, 'Knock, knock.' I just want to order a burger—was I supposed to say, 'Who's there?'"

Another time, as he was walking, a sighted person grabbed his shoulder without asking, screaming, "I'm a Christian, not a crook!"

Almost weekly he had incidents with Uber drivers standing him up or grilling him about his blindness. Sometimes bus people would hold his hand and pray over him so he could get his sight. He would laugh about it sometimes, and other times I could almost hear him shake his head.

And he heard me and listened to my work stories; I shared my own challenges, and he gave feedback or a welcomed listening ear. In his role as an audience to an advocate, he was sharing more with me.

We started a Facebook group discussion together. He led that group with a quiet leadership. I would run ideas by him, and he would share what worked and what didn't work.

We would talk about how some shows worked great, and why others didn't. Those conversations were hours long! We started to find some similarities, some core elements, and that gave us a nice shorthand to make our conversations easier.

"Ugh, Roy, the writing. Why are there so many prepositions together in that sentence that takes forever?"

Or "Kevin, what do you think about that narrator?"

And he'd say, "I didn't—I was totally into the story."

"Got it – the way she read the script; you were immersed in the story."

"YES!" he shouted, and I could hear him laugh and exhale. "Roy. If I have to turn my volume up and down any more times in this show…"

"Kevin, I know, that show needs a sound engineer."

"Kevin! Did you hear the audio description on that new show?"

Then there would be a long pause. "Nooooooo…" it was a guttural, do-not-mess-with-me tone. His fists clenching his phone.

And when I asked if AD should pass from cinema to streaming? He shouted, "YES!" And he turned on some Annie Lennox music.

We talked about connecting audio description audiences with the entertainment industry. "An awards show! Or Oscars for audio description! What about the Emmys, Roy, can you do that? I'll come to the parties. Have Snapple and Gummi Bears at your house, please."

What could we do to start connecting? What organizations could we reach? How could they work together? I found myself using my phone headset more often so I could pace around my room, our shared energy pulsing between the long-distance connection.

We kept talking on our unlimited phone plans. Our text messages had no character limit.

When I reread our Facebook messages on my laptop, I swipe vertically. It takes me back in time, the scroll bar of our chats shrinking as I never quite seem to reach the top. The block responses of my blue and his white stretch longer and wider.

She said Sunday morning he played his music. That was his time. His mother didn't mess with him.

She said she was sad when she found him.

I found out on Facebook where we met. Several close friends of his sent a private message asking to connect with me. I was so used to reaching him when I had something important to share that my first thought was to call him and tell him I'm so sorry.

———

I had spent months working on this organization that would find solutions to the challenges that we had spent years talking about—and was close to announcing it in a keynote speech for the American Council of the Blind. But I couldn't come up with a name for it. I thought of combining his Juneteenth birthday and his initials as a name, but it sounded like a license plate.

That's when my business advisor offered a simple title for now—a placeholder—that told the story of what the business would be. He suggested that blind people would come up with the best name.

So, the name "Kevin's Way" will work as a placeholder for now.

Made in the USA
Columbia, SC
27 November 2024

47258261R00098